OSPREY COMBAT AIRCRAFT • 54

C-47/R4D UNITS
IN THE
ETO AND MTO

SERIES EDITOR: TONY HOLMES

OSPREY COMBAT AIRCRAFT • 54

C-47/R4D UNITS IN THE ETO AND MTO

DAVID ISBY

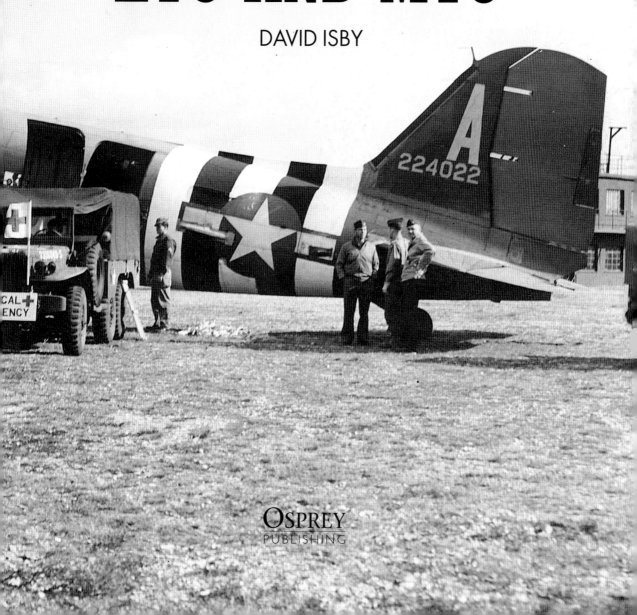

OSPREY
PUBLISHING

Front cover

On the night of 11 July 1943, veteran C-47 41-38704 *Geronimo* of the 36th Troop Carrier Squadron/316th Troop Carrier Group was loaded for Operation *Husky 2* – the follow-up US airdrop on Sicily, carrying men of the 504th Parachute Infantry Regimental Combat Team. Its pilot was Capt James R Farris, squadron operations officer, with 2Lt Joseph P Baxter as his co-pilot.

As the C-47 formation overflew the US invasion fleet, *Geronimo's* crew flashed their recognition lights, then fired the colours of the day from a Very pistol. Nevertheless, the American ships opened fire and *Geronimo* was hit repeatedly. Shell fragments ripped off the rear fuselage door and a shell damaged the left stabiliser. Other C-47s in the formation were also hit, and one exploded in mid-air. Several were trailing flames as their pilots tried to ditch in an effort to save the paratroopers.

Farris and Baxter opened the throttles and dove *Geronimo* for the deck, picking up speed and hoping to escape the hail of gunfire as they hauled the heavy C-47 into a violent turn to escape searchlights. Then they saw, dead ahead, a parapack – a bundle of ammunition or other heavy cargo – that had been jettisoned from another C-47 trying to escape the naval gunfire. Farris pulled *Geronimo* into a tight turn, hanging on the edge of a stall. Both pilots turned just in time for the parapack to miss the cockpit but smash through the fuselage aft of the astrodome. It steamrollered its way through the paratroopers and then fell out of the wildly turning *Geronimo* through where the two rear doors had been, followed by its shroud lines and parachute.

After the collision, according to Farris, 'The aeroplane spun at a right angle and nearly pulled the controls from my grasp. For a second I didn't realise what had happened. Then, finding myself out of formation, I began a violent evasive action. I saw three C-47s burning on the ground and red tracers everywhere as the gunners sprayed us as if potting flight ducks. Meanwhile, I had to cut into a less dangerous spot to give the paratroopers a fighting chance to reach the ground. After dropping the paratroopers, we tried to sneak out to sea again, but they kept shooting at us for 15 minutes longer'.

Geronimo returned to its Tunisian base at low altitude. Upon landing, Baxter went back to inspect the damage. It seemed to him that half of the aircraft was missing, yet the C-47's strength and ruggedness had saved the crew. *Geronimo* made it back to base, but damaged beyond repair, it was cannibalised for spares. Farris, promoted to major and in command of the 36th TCS, was killed in a mid-air collision in England in May 1944 during the D-Day airborne invasion rehearsal, Operation *Eagle* (*Cover artwork by Mark Postlethwaite*)

First published in Great Britain in 2005 by Osprey Publishing
1st Floor Elms Court, Chapel Way, Botley, Oxford, OX2 9LP

ISBN 1 84176 750 6

Edited by Tony Holmes
Page design by Tony Truscott
Cover Artwork by Mark Postlethwaite
Aircraft Profiles by Chris Davey
Scale Drawings by Mark Styling
Index by Alan Thatcher
Originattion by Grasmere Digital Imaging, Leeds, UK
Printed in China through Bookbuilders Hong Kong

05 06 07 08 09   10 09 08 07 06 05 04 03 02 01

CONTENTS

ORIGINS

In 1941, the US Army Air Corps (USAAC) and the US Navy, both
unprepared for war, adopted as a transport the Douglas DC-3, an
aircraft designed for peaceful commerce. In the years that followed,
these services used the aircraft to demonstrate that the air was a way to
project power, for armies to move or allies to be supplied, as had been
done by land and sea for centuries. Army Air Force C-47/53s and Navy
R4Ds (the military versions of the DC-3) made this possible.

American airliners of the early 1930s introduced the future of aviation
– all-metal, stressed skin aluminum construction, retractable landing
gear, reliable and powerful cowled engines, cantilever monoplane wings,
constant-speed propellers, de-icer boots, flaps and radio navigation aids.
Although the Boeing 247 had all of these features, Transcontinental and
Western Airlines (TWA) asked Douglas Aircraft for a better airliner. The
resulting prototype DC-1 (Douglas Commercial) first flew on 1 July
1933. An enlarged version went into production in 1934 as the DC-2 and
proved successful worldwide. Improvements in engine technology, and a
need for an aeroplane capable of handling transcontinental journeys in
the US, saw the DC-2 evolve into the Douglas Sleeper Transport (DST)
in December 1935 and then, in 1936, the DC-3.

The DC-3, bigger and more powerful than its predecessors, could fly
passengers profitably – without a government subsidy – throughout the
US in all weathers. The DC-3 was developed by airline money. Its early-
1930s technology structure, enlarged from that of the DC-1, provided
strength at the expense of performance. But improved loads, volume and
range were made possible by 1050 hp Pratt & Whitney radials. The
DC-3 was big and powerful enough to be militarily significant, both as a
bomber (the DC-2 inspired B-18 Bolo) and as a transport.

SERVICE BACKGROUND

In the 1930s, transport aircraft were a low priority for the ill funded
USAAC and Navy. Transport units were limited to small detachments
flying priority cargo and passengers, although the Marines were using a
few transports in combat in Nicaragua. Both services realised that
without transports to support them, their combat aircraft would have
only a limited ability to operate from dispersed bases, or to deploy to US
overseas possessions. Maj Hugh J Knerr, chief of the field service section
of the USAAC Material Division, started an air resupply system and
urged the procurement of transport aircraft.

The military and the growing airline industry shared close links to the
aircraft industry. Indeed, many airline pilots were reservists, and the
services learned from airlines how emerging technologies revolutionised
aviation.

The 1934 Baker Board (chaired by former Secretary of War Newton
Baker) highlighted civil aviation advances, and advocated adopting
modified airliners. The USAAC had wanted specially designed large

The first modern USAAC transport, the C-33 was a modified version of the DC-2 airliner that had been adapted to carry military cargo (*AAHS from Karol W Vardel*)

cargo carriers, but the Baker Board was embraced by USAAC chief Brig Gen Oscar Westover in 1933, ordering modified airliners.

In 1934-35, the Navy received five standard DC-2s (two for the Marines) under the designation R2D-1 – the first US military procurement of a modern transport. Westover, after acquiring one DC-2 as the VIP-configured XC-32, ordered 11 examples of the C-33 (the military version of the DC-2, with a large two-piece side cargo door in the port aft fuselage and a reinforced cabin deck). C-33s were deployed in small numbers for priority cargo – especially spare engines – and supporting combat aircraft deployments. Despite minimal resources – in August 1937 Secretary of War Henry Woodring decided the transport role could be filled by obsolete bombers – the USAAC slowly started to acquire aircraft to match its thinking. The 10th Transport Group (TG) as activated in 1937 as the first permanent airlift unit.

Following a few DC-2-based C-34s and C-38s, 35 C-39s (a DC-2/DST hybrid), which retained the C-33's cargo door, were delivered in 1937. Some C-39s joined the C-33s dispersed in support roles, while others were organised into multi-role transport squadrons. The USAAC hesitated to order a military version of the DC-3 even though it was, by 1939, coming off the production line in increasing numbers for the world's airlines. USAAC chief Gen Henry 'Hap' Arnold emphasised the procurement of combat aircraft, especially those intended for strategic bombing – transports could be ordered 'off the shelf' in a crisis.

NEW MISSIONS AND AIRCRAFT

What changed the USAAC's priorities on transport aircraft were the spring 1940 German offensives. The Luftwaffe, learning the lessons of Spanish Civil War airlifts, had realised the importance of transport aircraft before the more technologically advanced Americans. In Norway and the Netherlands, German paratroopers and glider troops had seized airfields, while follow-on sorties flew in reinforcements.

In September 1940, the USAAC ordered a military DC-3 with a large cargo door and reinforced cabin flooring, designated the C-47, along with a personnel transport version without the enlarged door, designated the C-53. The USAAC also ordered airline-configured DC-3s off the assembly lines, and impressed others already in airline service. The Navy placed orders for the R4D, its own C-47 version.

The forward cockpit and instrument panel of a standard C-47 (*National Archives*)

An early-production C-53 – basically identical to a DC-3, minus a baggage hatch – of the 10th TG immediately prior to the surprise attack on Pearl Harbor (*National Archives*)

Both services also placed orders for larger and more capable transport versions of airliner designs that represented 1941 high technology. The USAAC ordered twin-engined Curtiss C-46s and four-engined Douglas C-54s, while the Navy ordered twin-engined Douglas R3Ds, which was a version of the DC-5 airliner. Specially designed military transports were soon on manufacturers' drawing boards.

But these could not replace the C-47. Because, in part, of problems encountered with other designs, and reluctance to assign resource priority to transport acquisition, the C-47 was used for a range of wartime missions. It was not the most advanced or best suited design, but it was proven and available.

New aircraft would need new units. The USAAC formed the 50th Transport Wing (TW), grouping together previously scattered aircraft. In December 1940, most USAAC transport squadrons were pulled together into the first of a new type of combat unit – the troop carrier group. At the end of 1940, the USAAC had only 122 transports, mainly small and obsolescent aircraft. Plans called for the establishment of six transport groups and 18 transport squadrons. All were formed, albeit on paper, by February 1941.

Before Pearl Harbor, the US Army Air Forces' (the USAAC had been renamed in June 1941) C-47s, and other military transports, were already committed to intratheatre transport, troop carrier missions in support of airborne forces and long-range intertheatre transport missions. But only 133 transports were delivered in 1941 – 66 C-47/53s were in service as of October 1941.

By mid-1942, over 11,000 twin-engined transports, mainly C-47s, were on order. C-47 production lagged due to low priority for resources. This also applied to trained personnel, as C-47 units were often short-handed, receiving reinforcements only in response to urgent needs. Other military orders delayed C-47s (and all but the initial C-53s) produced at Douglas' original Santa Monica factory, and a factory was set up at Long Beach. By 1942 these plants were at the limits of their capacity. A new plant at Tulsa, Oklahoma, was built, production starting in 1943.

THE RISE OF AIR TRANSPORT COMMAND

A global war demanded worldwide air links from the US to deliver aircraft, cargo and personnel. After the fall of France in 1940, US airliners pioneered flights to the combat zones, with the stars-and-

stripes optimistically painted large to protect them as neutrals. The DC-3 was not designed for routine intercontinental flights but as C-54s would not appear in significant numbers until 1943-44, they would have to carry the long-haul burden, supplemented by flying boats and a few modified bombers.

In March 1941, the British requested the delivery of US-built aircraft directly to Egypt. Two months later the USAAC formed Ferry Command to deliver aircraft to lend-lease and US military destinations. Airline personnel under contract supplemented its former airline personnel in uniform.

Supporting the British in the Middle East required a transatlantic route from Miami – a southern Atlantic crossing from Brazil, refuelling at Ascension Island, then cross Africa to Cairo. With the US (and Brazil) still neutral, Pan American Airways started aircraft deliveries in June 1941, followed by DC-3 air transport services from 21 October.

After Pearl Harbor, the USAAF had a seemingly infinite requirement for high-priority shipments both to the US and overseas. In May 1942, the USAAF impressed many of the remaining airline DC-2s and DC-3s. Only 200 DC-3s remained in airline livery for high-priority domestic passenger and freight work.

With crews trained for long-range missions remaining scarce, airline-manned aircraft carried out missions before their military counterparts were ready. USAAF C-47/53s were operated by airlines under contract on the northern route to Britain, via US bases in Labrador and Iceland. Pan American started flying C-53s from Miami to Brazil in February 1942, being joined by Eastern Airlines in May. At the same time, Northeast Airlines received contracts for the northern route, flying impressed DC-3s and C-53s to Goose Bay, Newfoundland, Iceland and Scotland. American Airlines, flying to Iceland, joined them.

USAAF C-47/53s of Ferry Command were assigned the southern route to Africa in early 1942, allowing Pan American to turn its DC-3s over to the RAF. Some USAAF C-47s (and C-32s) flew on to India. Others were based in Egypt.

Ferry Command (renamed Air Transport Command in June 1942) was under the command of Brig (later Lt) Gen Harold George, (who was to remain its CO throughout the war) with his deputy commander for operations Col C R Smith (who as CEO of

The ATC had to create an infrastructure along its external routes where previously there had been none, or very little. This was often viewed by local administrators, and by officials in London, as US interference. This is an aerial view of the ATC facility at Accra, Gold Coast, in 1944, showing at least 14 C-47s on the ground (*National Archives*)

This DC-3 was impressed as a C-49C (one of two ex-Delta Airlines) or C-49D (11 ex-Eastern Airlines) model, powered by Wright Cyclone engines (*National Archives*)

American Airlines had ordered the DST). The ATC at first organised three wings – Caribbean, South Atlantic, and Africa-Middle East – committed to the southern route. After several pioneering flights using airline personnel on the northern route to Iceland and Prestwick from Labrador, the ATC started operating that as well.

In addition to experienced airline crews, the ATC offered commissions to qualified pilots – barnstormers, crop dusters and Great War veterans – scorned by the 'real' USAAF. These volunteers dubbed the ATC the 'Airline of Terrified Civilians'. In many cases, it would be years before base facilities and navigation aids were established on their routes.

ATC transports worldwide would respond to orders directly from 'Hap' Arnold in Washington. Local commanders could not divert ATC transports – including those used for intratheatre missions – for their own use except in cases of grave emergency.

NAVAL AIR TRANSPORT SERVICE

By the time of Pearl Harbor, the US Navy's Atlantic Fleet had effectively been at war for almost a year. It needed increased air transport support at bases from Iceland to Brazil. As the US Navy's first R4D-1 order was obviously too small, the re-allocation of C-47/53s ordered for the USAAF to the Navy (and Marines) was approved – an arrangement that would continue till war's end.

R4Ds of the Naval Air Transport Service (NATS) Atlantic Wing started operations in February 1942. In Iceland, Newfoundland and other remote bases, convoy escorts had replacements or new radar sets flown to them, while injured sailors were evacuated.

THE AIRBORNE MISSION

While the US had planned airborne forces in 1918, and was aware of Soviet experiments in the 1930s, it was the German victories of 1940 (and British emulation) that led the

DC-3s operated by Pan American opened up the southern transatlantic route from the US, across Africa, to Cairo before Pearl Harbor. Ferry Command DC-3s continued this vital mission – the fastest way to get priority shipments to the desert was by fast ship to West Africa and then by DC-3 – until after Brazil joined the war. This DC-3, photographed in 1942, has lost its airline titles and US flag and acquired an RAF fin flash instead (*National Archives*)

An echelon of NATS R4Ds formate for the camera off Miami. When the U-boats moved into the Caribbean in mid-1942 following their successes off the US east coast, USAAF and Navy ASW aircraft, deployed to airstrips throughout the region, depended on R4D resupply to remain operational (*National Archives*)

US Army to organise its first para-chute test platoon in July 1940, jumping from B-18 bombers. The first US Army airborne battalion, the 501st, was organised in September 1940, followed by three more battalions. These were expanded to regiments in 1941.

In June 1941, the 50th TG – heavily committed to transport missions throughout the Western hemisphere – scraped hard to gather 12 aircraft for a company-sized airdrop in the Louisiana manoeuvres. In August 1941, joint-air ground exercises in Panama showed the importance of transport support to forward-deployed aircraft, and identified problems in air-ground coordination that would take years to resolve. In November 1941, a maximum effort by the 50th TW pulled together 39 transports – C-32s, C-33s, C-39s, C-48s and the first C-53 – for the first US multi-company airdrop and a follow-on air-landing echelon at the Maxson, North Carolina, municipal airport. This success led to the formation of the 82nd and 101st Airborne Divisions in 1942. The Navy and Marines also soon committed their transports to this role, the latter forming parachute and raider battalions. R4Ds soon took over from the few R3Ds.

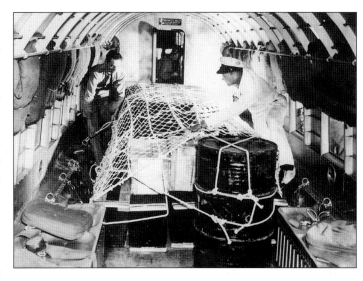

A mixed cargo is lashed in place inside a NATS R4D, showing the metal bucket seats common to many wartime C-47 series aircraft, replacing the canvas sling types on earlier production models. Many C-47s flew with these seats removed (*National Archives*)

I TROOP CARRIER COMMAND

The new USAAF I Troop Carrier Command – spun off from the Air Service Command in June 1942 – had as a cadre re-designated pre-war transport units (unlike the ATC, created largely from airline assets). With the formation of I TCC, all 12 stateside Transport Groups became Troop Carrier Groups, while the 50th Transport Wing became the 50th Troop Carrier Wing. The primary troop carrier mission was the insertion and sustainment of airborne forces, with a secondary mission of intratheatre air transport in support of US air or ground forces.

Throughout 1942-44, the USAAF formed and I TCC trained C-47-equipped Troop Carrier Groups in the US. In 1942, the number of these

Paratroopers of Company G, 502nd Parachute Infantry Regiment at Fort Bragg get ready for the jump into Maxson airport on 28 November 1941. Their rifles and ammunition would be dropped in separate containers. The C-53 of the 63rd TG is marked with the red cross that denoted 'enemy' forces during the Carolina manoeuvres (*National Archives*)

groups had been capped at 12, resulting in a rush to organise new groups later. Most started off with a handful of various types of trans-ports, and few met the 1941 organisation of three 12-aeroplane squadrons per group. In 1942, this was increased to four 13-aeroplane squadrons per group (the 13th C-47 was a group asset attached for maintenance or as a spare).

Of the squadron's 12 aircraft, nine had to be available for combat

Paratroopers jump from C-53 41-20074 of the 62nd TG (as it was then designated) in early 1942. This aircraft remained in the US on training and transport duties throughout the war. Note static lines from previous jumpers trailing from the door (*National Archives*)

operations. C-53s, which were always limited in numbers, would be mixed in for personnel transport duties, frequently at group-level.

I TCC developed tactics for dropping paratroops and supplies, towing gliders and operating unarmed and unarmoured transports in combat. Troop carrier crews were trained in evasive action against fighters, including using their slipstream to catch an attacker.

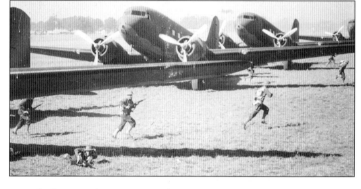

As part of the airborne phase of the last pre-war Carolina manoeuvres, reinforcements of the 9th Infantry Regiment are flown into an airhead seized by paratroopers. This basic scenario – based on German experience – was planned for, but never repeated, in the ETO/MTO (*National Archives*)

C-47s would drop paratroopers from 500 ft, flying at slow cruise speed in three-ship vee and nine-ship squadron formations, flying in trail in larger serials usually of up to 36-48 aircraft, all heading for the same drop zone (DZ). To keep the paratroopers together, there would be no evasive action. While dropping supplies – usually from 350 ft – allowed a larger envelope of performance, C-47s dropping paratroops were extremely vulnerable to enemy action. A C-47 could carry only 18-22 fully armed and equipped paratroopers at an operational range. A parachute infantry battalion (PIB) required 36-45 C-47s flying a tight formation, and the troops could be dropped in two minutes in a 1000 x 500 yard DZ.

The US followed the Germans and British in adopting gliders to deliver troops, supplies, artillery and vehicles. The Waco CG-4A was selected for mass-production as the standard USAAF combat glider, and troop carrier groups learned to tow gliders – an integral part of each group – and to snatch them up again from their landing zone (LZ). But in 1942-43, some groups deployed without glider towing capabilities, while other groups deployed without having dropped paratroops.

The basic glider towing formation was the two-aircraft echelon, with two of these flying together. These formations flew in trail in larger serials, all heading for the same LZ. In training, it was demonstrated that a C-47 could tow two loaded CG-4As simultaneously.

A diagram of the standard USAAC/USAAF vee-of-vees formation used by troop carrier squadrons for paratroop delivery

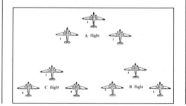

INTO BATTLE

In the summer of 1942, the first Troop Carrier Groups were ordered to deploy, although their training – especially in formation flying and long-range navigation – was weak and aircraft (only 524 C-47/53s in total) were scarce. First to move off on the North Atlantic route to England were 150 C-47s of the 60th, 62nd and 64th TCGs (what would become Col Paul L Williams' 51st TCW) on 26 August, 1942. They were hastily fitted with cabin tanks for ferrying.

The 60th was in the best shape, but it had only 27 of 52 C-47s and 36 out of 60 navigators (all but one fresh out of training). It did better in pilots, with 18 having over 1000 hours to their credit. The other groups were not as fortunate. They had less of a cadre, and their pilots arrived straight from training units to fly the North Atlantic. Before arriving in England, the 60th TCG was used to carry supplies to the bases being built on the North Atlantic route.

The 51st TCW became part of the Eighth Air Force, originally intended for a 1943 invasion of Europe. But on arrival in England they were committed to training for the invasion of French North Africa. The first US paratroopers to deploy overseas joined them.

Three C-47s – part of VIII Air Force Service Command (AFSC) – were being used for transport duties in Britain months before the Eighth Air Force flew its first combat mission in August 1942. The Eighth's bomber and fighter groups were based in eastern England, and with its main depots near ports in Northern Ireland and Lancashire, it required airlift support. VIII AFSC had 12 C-47s by December 1942, supplemented by Troop Carrier Group C-47s, including two squadrons of the 315th TCG following their arrival in England in December 1942.

C-47 41-18347 of the 64th TCG is overflown by three aircraft undertaking a training flight in England in the autumn of 1942. Delivered to the USAAF on 17 May 1942, this particular aircraft survived North Africa and Sicily before being withdrawn from use in Italy on 6 November 1943 after suffering battle damage (*National Archives*)

Paratroopers of the 503rd PIR prepare to climb aboard 60th TCG C-47 41-7824 prior to Operation *Torch*. Although bearing yellow-ringed roundels for the invasion, this aircraft did not participate in the initial *Torch* mission, flying to North Africa later in the campaign. Delivered to the USAAF on 26 April 1942, and initially serving with the 317th TG, it was lost in a mid-air collision on 11 July 1943 during the invasion of Sicily (*National Archives*)

EGYPT

Some 12 USAAF transports – impressed DC-2/3s, C-47/53s – were in Egypt by the summer of 1942, committed to priority intratheatre transport and casualty evacuation missions. They flew to forward landing strips and RAF bases throughout the Middle East, where they were joined by transports pulled back from India. ATC despatched more C-47s to Cairo.

This early-production C-53 transport (basically a DC-3 without airline fittings, and with gunports in the fuselage windows) is seen carrying out a casualty evacuation mission for the British Eighth Army at a forward desert airstrip in the early autumn of 1942. These transports were among the first US-marked aircraft to be committed to the North African campaign, preceding the arrival of the 316th TCG in November 1942. Some were later transferred to the RAF as Dakota Is, while others flew on to the China-Burma-India theatre (*National Archives*)

These aircraft, operated by the US Middle East Air Force (soon re-designated the Ninth Air Force) AFSC, were reinforced when the 316th TCG commenced operations in Egypt in November 1942, having flown from its training fields in Texas via the southern route. Its 52 C-47s helped the victorious Desert Air Force move forward to abandoned Axis bases. On 11-12 December, for example, six of the 316th's C-47s flew over 11,000 gallons of aviation fuel to desert landing grounds near Tobruk, returning with 77 casualties. These missions were repeated time and time again during the British advance towards Tunisia, fortunately with only one C-47 lost to the *Afrika Korps*.

OPERATION *TORCH*

The invasion of Vichy French North Africa in November 1942 – simultaneous amphibious strikes at Casablanca, in Morocco, and Oran and Algiers, in Algeria – required the French airfields of La Senia and Tafaraoui, near Oran, to be seized as fighter bases. This became the mission of the US Parachute Task Force, training in England.

Col William Bentley lead 39 C-47s of his 60th TCG, carrying Maj Edson Raff's 2nd Battalion, 503rd Parachute Infantry Regiment (2-503rd PIR). Taking off from RAF St Eval and Predannack on 7 November, they flew directly to La Senia, which was reportedly controlled by pro-Allied French troops. There had been no mission rehearsals, and a lack of pilots meant 14 replacements from Eighth Air Force units had to be found at the last minute. The 60th's hastily trained navigators were issued with unfamiliar RAF equipment and charts.

The formation would home in on a radio beacon on a warship offshore. Navigational direction to the target would be provided by a covert radar beacon, operated by an agent – so secret, it did not then even have a codename! To receive it, a few of the 60th's C-47s were hastily fitted with the secret forward-facing antenna arrays of what later became known as the Rebecca/Eureka system.

The longest-range air assault of the war (1100 miles) came close to disaster. Flying through the night of 7-8 November in cloud at 10,000 ft, three C-47s were forced to land in neutral Spain – one left its paratroopers behind to lighten the load, then flew on to Algeria – two had to land in French Morocco and another diverted to Gibraltar with engine trouble. French fighters forced three more to land en route. The radio and radar beacons failed to operate.

The remaining 28 C-47s arrived near La Senia on the morning of 8 November, where they were met by anti-aircraft fire. Two crash-landed and French fighters forced three more down. Their fuel exhausted, the C-47s landed wherever looked safe, most on a nearby dry lake bed. Some paratroops jumped and took up defensive positions.

Following further Vichy air attacks, and learning that the US Army held the nearby Tafaraoui military airfield, some of the remaining flyable C-47s lifted paratroopers there. USAAF fighters intercepted them, fortunately without loss. Vichy fighters and artillery fire knocked out more C-47s, leaving only 14 aircraft flyable and 150 paratroopers ready for follow-on missions on 10 November. The Parachute Task Force had failed to accomplish its objectives, fortunately with light casualties.

Amongst the crews from the 60th TCG taking part in this action was the 12th TCS's Capt John G Evans, piloting C-47 41-7764. Leading 'C' flight, his aircraft was carrying paratroopers from Easy Company 2-503rd PIR. The remaining crewmen in Evans' C-47 were 2Lt Jack B Goudy (co-pilot), 2Lt Julius A La Croix (navigator), Sgt Howard J Ryerson (engineer) and Sgt Joseph O'Neale (radio). Evans recalled;

'Forty minutes after take-off, we lost our wingman, Lt Litsey, in Ship 42 (he landed in Spanish Morocco). We were No 3 in a four-ship element (Tobler was leading and Swartz was No 2), and had great difficulty in holding formation because of poor visibility. However, we managed to hang on until we reached a point one hour from our destination. All three ships went their separate ways at this point, weather making formation flying both extremely dangerous and humanly impossible.

'At the time of separation, we were flying a course of 170 degrees. I had no trouble in turning in on (shipboard) radio marker X, and after taking a bearing I turned to 95 degrees and held this course for an hour.

'At the end of that time it was 0606 hrs, with light fast beginning to come. We picked up the boat at X in good shape, but absolutely no other C-47s were to be seen. We circled for ten minutes, and in one sweep came within range of three of our own sea transports next to the beach west of Oran. They gave us a warm reception, with tracers falling way short of us.

'We then entered the dry lake area, with intentions of proceeding to our landing field. It was soon evident that there was plenty of trouble on the ground – gun flashes all along the northern slope of the area. Upon approaching within three miles of Tafaraoui airfield, we were greeted with some genuine ack ack, unpleasantly close. We turned 180 degrees and poured it on. Some seconds later we spotted a second ship – Maj Galligan's. I told him the general situation on C channel but got no reply.

'Suddenly from above and behind, all hell broke loose. Tracers cut through us like mad. Then the Frenchie (Vichy Dewoitine D 520 fighter) went shooting by, climbing for another run on us. We were then at about 7000 ft, climbing. I cut the power, half-rolled and dove for the ground, levelling out at over the airspeed indicators' range just above the ground.

'Frenchie came in again as I levelled off. I pulled up sharply and directly toward him. He wheeled off without getting a shot home. Again I dove, calling for wheels at the same time. We were on the ground, indicating 165, in no time. We slowed and I ground looped so as to get a view of Frenchie again. He was some distance out, turning in for another run. Everybody was out of the ship before he opened fire this time, but Ryerson was wounded twice in the arm and got some explosive fragments near one eye. Frenchie made one more pass on us after that, finishing off the ship in pretty good shape.

'I dressed Ryerson's wounds with the first aid materials, Le Croix having dashed back to the ship for them. The we began to gather and organise. Maj Wanamaker landed beside us within five minutes, and we loaded all salvage from my ship and the balance of the crew aboard. The paratroopers stayed behind with me.

'Later that afternoon we were picked up by Capt Heins and landed at Tafaraoui in time for that unforgettable field artillery barrage. Two paratroop guards were left at my ship with our Vickers machine gun set up and water for three days. They were picked up later by marching paratroopers and ordered by higher authority within their organisation to go with them, I understand.'

On 9 November, 51st TCW commander Col Paul Williams led 39 C-47s of the 64th TCG from St Eval to Gibraltar carrying the British 3rd Battalion, the Parachute Regiment (3 Para). Some 34 C-47s landed at Senia on 11 November, flying through inaccurate Allied anti-aircraft fire.

Follow-up drops on the route to Tunis were ordered. The next day – the 64th was not trained for night drops – 312 British paratroops were dropped by 26 of its C-47s at Bone. On 12 November, the surviving C-47s from the 60th TCG, now operating from Algiers' Maison Blanche airport, dropped 350 US paratroopers at Youks-les-Bains airfield in a hastily improvised, yet successful, mission. In another hastily planned effort, 32 C-47s of the 64th successfully dropped 384 British paratroopers at Souk-el-Arab on 16 November without loss (after the mission had been scrubbed the previous day due to weather). By then, however, German troops, airlifted in Ju 52/3ms, had seized ports in Tunisia, thus ensuring a lengthy campaign.

TUNISIAN CAMPAIGN

As part of the 'race to Tunis', on 29 November 530 British paratroops of 2 Para were dropped over Depienne airfield. Flying in daylight, with RAF fighter escort, 44 C-47s – 26 of them from the newly arrived 62nd TCG – made the scattered airdrop. When the Allied forces intended to link up with 2 Para were forced to retreat, the paratroopers had to fight their way out, taking four days and suffering 50 per cent casualties.

On the night of 26 December, three C-47s of the 60th TCG carried 32 paratroopers to blow up a bridge near El Djem, in Tunisia. Making use of a full moon, the C-47s flew in formation to the DZ at low-altitude to avoid detection. However, the paratroopers became lost between the DZ and the objective and were captured.

Torch veteran Capt John G Evans was also involved in this mission, flying the second C-47 (41-7807) in the formation sent to El Djem – he had Lt Goudy as his co-pilot. Lt Col Lee of the 51st TCW HQ flew the lead ship, with Maj Williamson as co-pilot, and Capt E P Davis of the 11th TCS/60th TCG piloted the third C-47, with Lt Clerici as his co-pilot. Capt Evans provided to the following description of the mission;

'The formation was at all times to fly on the deck, pulling up only for the drop. Radio silence was observed, and no lights of any kind were to be shown. Take-off was set for the rise of the moon, about 2300 hrs (C-47 41-7828, flown by Capt Heins and Lt R D Smith, served as an on-ground spare).

'At 1700 hrs a reconnaissance flight was made by Maj Philip Cochran (who then flew the C-47 mission in the lead ship jumpseat) in a P-40 along the route of the proposed flight and the (*text continues on page 28*)

COLOUR PLATES

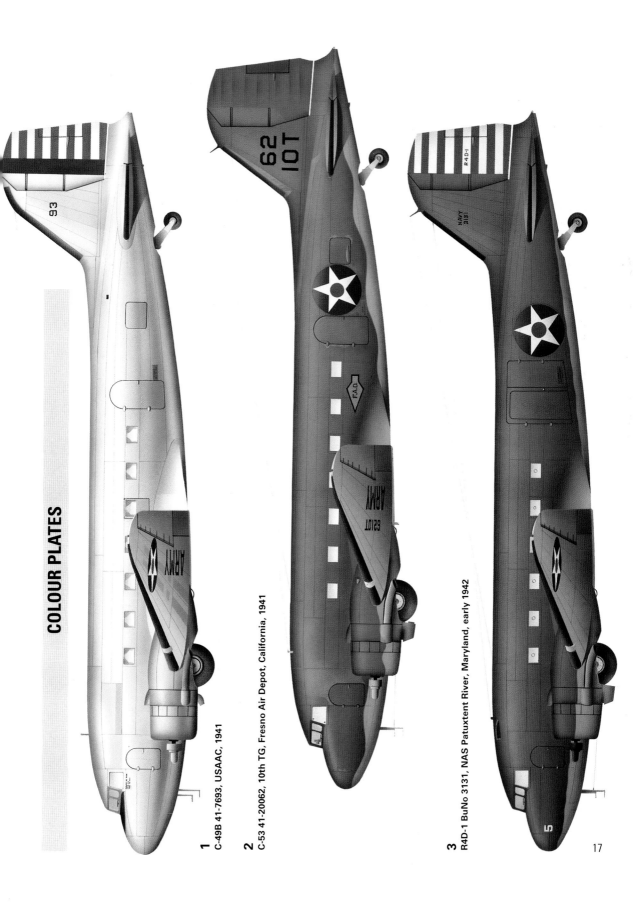

1
C-49B 41-7693, USAAC, 1941

2
C-53 41-20062, 10th TG, Fresno Air Depot, California, 1941

3
R4D-1 BuNo 3131, NAS Patuxent River, Maryland, early 1942

4
C-53-DO 41-20090, ATC, 1942

5
C-47-DL 41-38576, Accra, Gold Coast, 1942

6
C-47-DL 41-18608, 60th TCG, Huntingdon, Cambridgeshire, October 1942

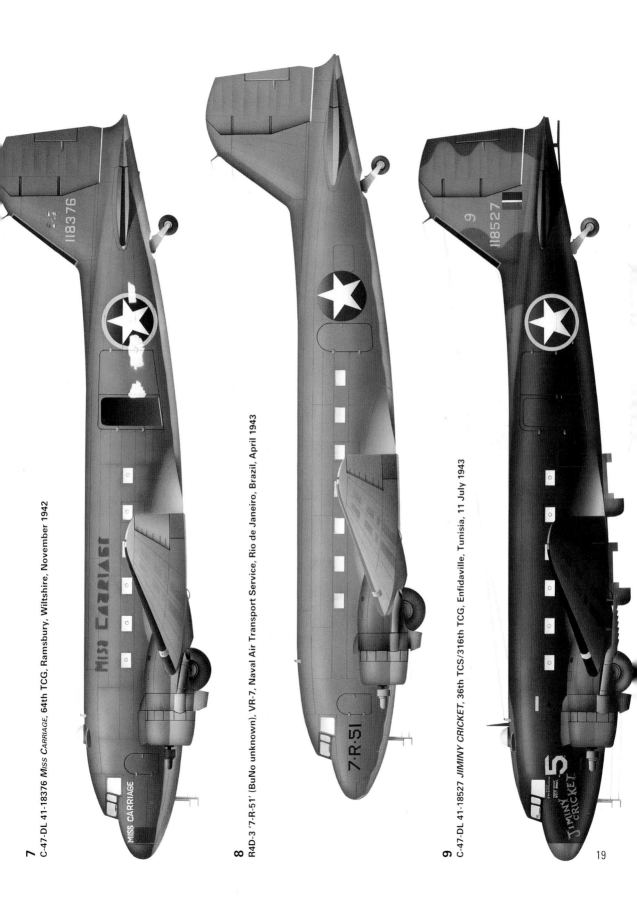

7
C-47-DL 41-18376 *MISS CARRIAGE*, 64th TCG, Ramsbury, Wiltshire, November 1942

8
R4D-3 '7-R-51' (BuNo unknown), VR-7, Naval Air Transport Service, Rio de Janeiro, Brazil, April 1943

9
C-47-DL 41-18527 *JIMINY CRICKET*, 36th TCS/316th TCG, Enfidaville, Tunisia, 11 July 1943

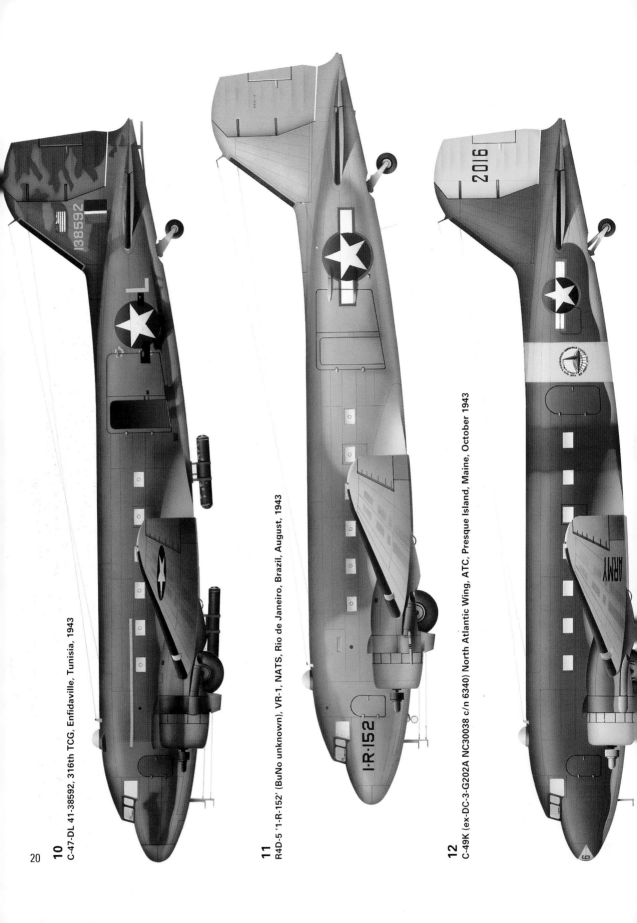

10
C-47-DL 41-38592, 316th TCG, Enfidaville, Tunisia, 1943

11
R4D-5 '1-R-152' (BuNo unknown), VR-1, NATS, Rio de Janeiro, Brazil, August, 1943

12
C-49K (ex-DC-3-G202A NC30038 c/n 6340) North Atlantic Wing, ATC, Presque Island, Maine, October 1943

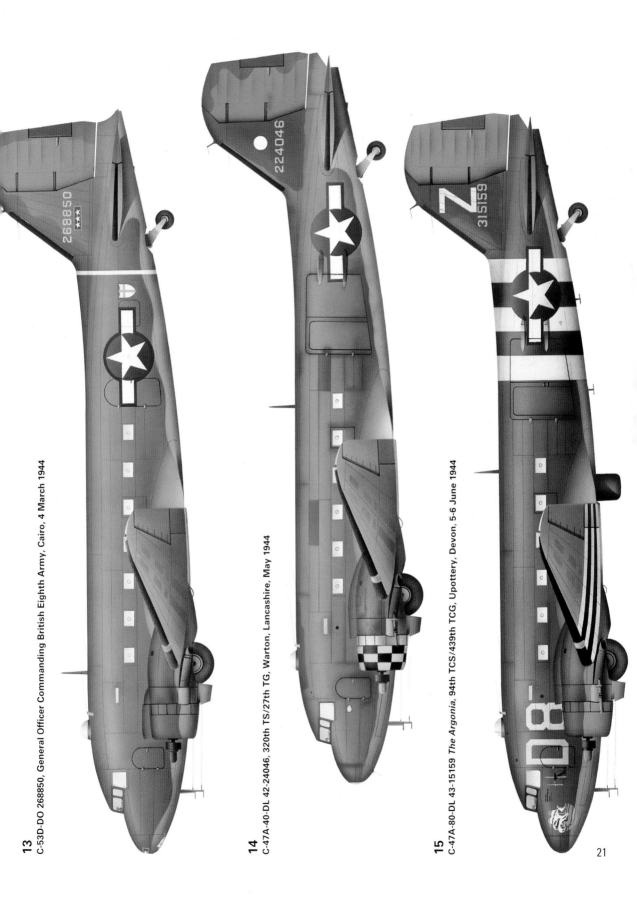

13
C-53D-DO 268850, General Officer Commanding British Eighth Army, Cairo, 4 March 1944

14
C-47A-40-DL 42-24046, 320th TS/27th TG, Warton, Lancashire, May 1944

15
C-47A-80-DL 43-15159 *The Argonia*, 94th TCS/439th TCG, Upottery, Devon, 5-6 June 1944

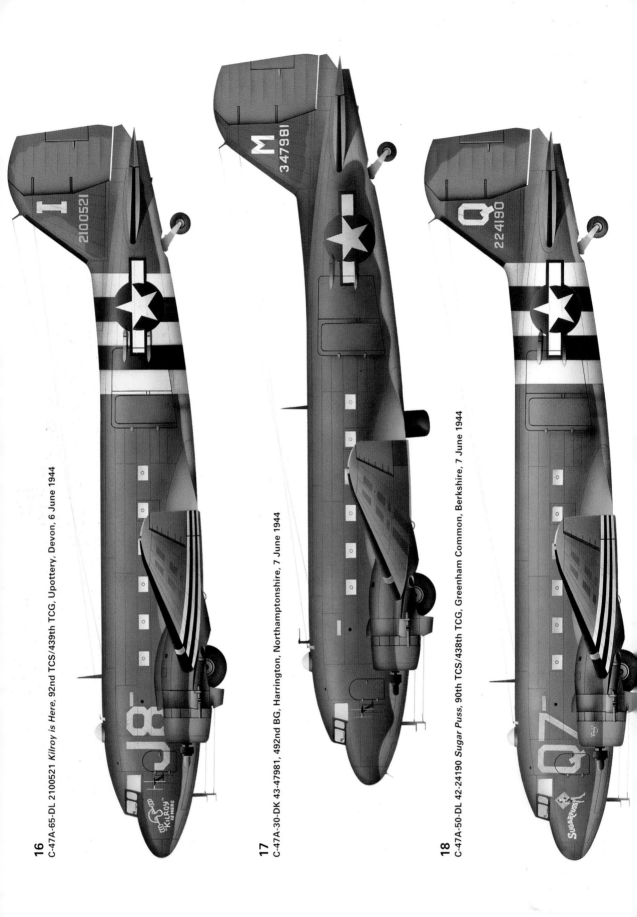

16
C-47A-65-DL 2100521 *Kilroy is Here*, 92nd TCS/439th TCG, Upottery, Devon, 6 June 1944

17
C-47A-30-DK 43-47981, 492nd BG, Harrington, Northamptonshire, 7 June 1944

18
C-47A-50-DL 42-24190 *Sugar Puss*, 90th TCS/438th TCG, Greenham Common, Berkshire, 7 June 1944

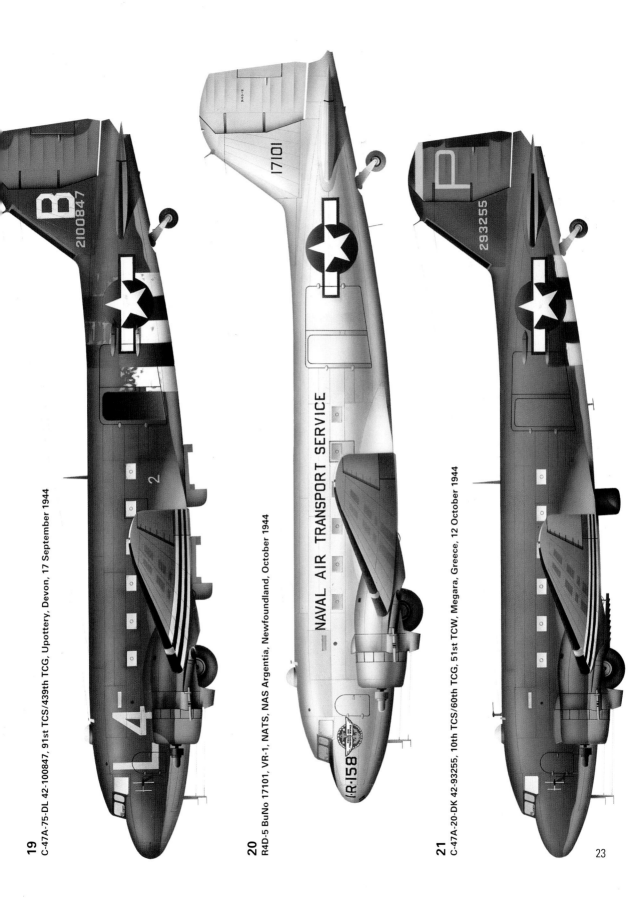

19
C-47A-75-DL 42-100847, 91st TCS/439th TCG, Upottery, Devon, 17 September 1944

20
R4D-5 BuNo 17101, VR-1, NATS, NAS Argentia, Newfoundland, October 1944

21
C-47A-20-DK 42-93255, 10th TCS/60th TCG, 51st TCW, Megara, Greece, 12 October 1944

22
C-47-DL 41-38607 *JACKPOT*, Headquarters Flight, Base Air Depot (BAD) 2, Warton, Lancashire, November 1944

23
C-47A-65-DL 42-100533 *Honeybun III*, 80th TCS/436th TCG, Membury, Berkshire, early 1945

24
C-47A-25-DK 42-93607, 79th TCS/436th TCG, Melun, France, March 1945

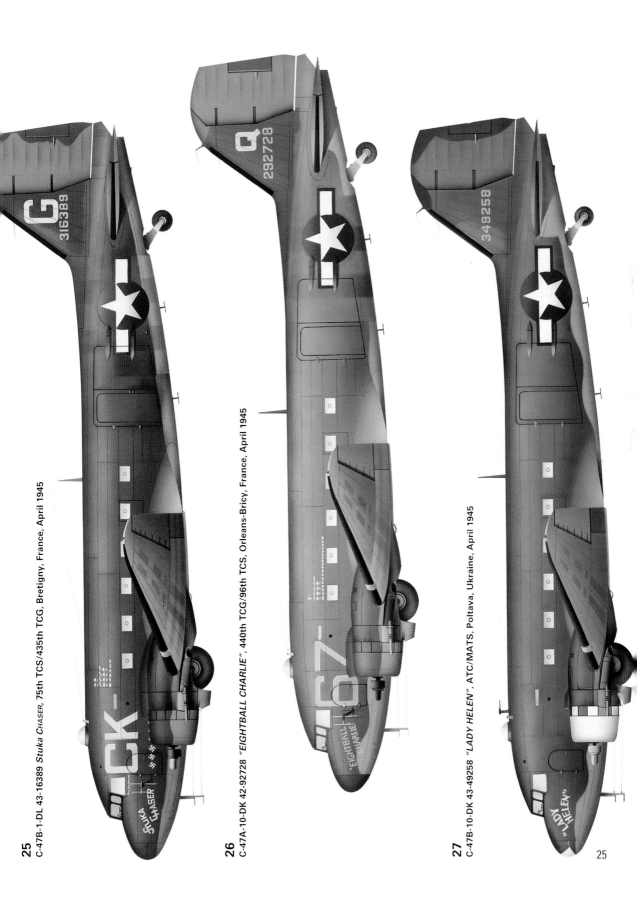

25
C-47B-1-DL 43-16389 *Stuka CHASER*, 75th TCS/435th TCG, Bretigny, France, April 1945

26
C-47A-10-DK 42-92728 *"EIGHTBALL CHARLIE"*, 440th TCG/96th TCS, Orleans-Bricy, France, April 1945

27
C-47B-10-DK 43-49258 *"LADY HELEN"*, ATC/MATS, Poltava, Ukraine, April 1945

28
C-47A-90-DL 43-15992 ATC, Orly, Paris, spring 1945

29
C-47B-1-DK 43-48474, 312th FS/27th TG, Villacoublay, France, spring 1945

30
C-47B-1-DK 43-48247 *Vandra Min Väg*, 86th TS/27th TG, Kierkenes, Norway, January-August 1945

1
C-47A-65-DL 2100521 *Kilroy is Here*, 92nd TCS/439th TCG, Upottery, Devon, 6 June 1944

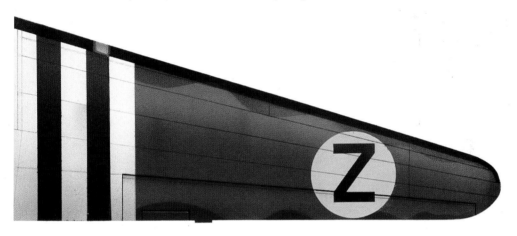

2
C-47A-80-DL 43-15159 *The Argonia*, 94th TCS/439th TCG, Upottery, Devon, 5-6 June 1944

3
R4D-5 BuNo 17101, VR-1, NATS, NAS Argentia, Newfoundland, October 1944

4
C-53-DO 41-20090, ATC, 1942

drop zone area. No heavy troop concentrations were noted. We were warned that some mobile flak might be expected along the route. The airfield at El Djem was rendered next to useless due to flood conditions, and only two or three fighters were noted there, hopelessly mired down. The bridge itself was guarded by what was believed to be a light force. This information was given to the paratroopers.

A Luftwaffe air attack on Biskra airfield on 15 January 1943 totally destroyed this C-47 (marked with pre-war national insignia), blowing it upside down (*National Archives*)

'The flight was calculated to take us 90 miles behind the enemy lines over the town of El Djem, and its adjacent airfield, to the bridge and back. The route passed within 20 km of an active, strong enemy air base. Because of the night operation, fighter protection was impractical, therefore not considered.

'At exactly 2303 hrs the three C-47s took off from Thelpete, Algeria, the most forward US air base, in close vee formation. The moon was full above the mountains to the northeast, and little scattered low clouds seemed only to brighten the night sky. I found that by flying some ten feet lower than the lead ship, thus keeping the dark hull of the ship silhouetted above the horizon, I was able to alleviate the strain on distance perception that always accompanied night formation flights.

'The flight to El Djem was accomplished perfectly according to plan, and it was exciting in that a heavy bombing raid was being made on Sousse harbour 20 miles north, and we were at ringside. I could envision the mobile flak battery hurrying up the road to help defend the harbour, and breathed a sigh of relief.

'We turned north directly over the airfield on the outskirts of El Djem and began pulling up and slowing down for the drop. We passed over the bridge in full view below us, and seconds later the Drop Zone was centred and all paratroopers and the three bundles (containing 500 lbs of TNT to destroy the bridge) got away in good order. It was the most perfect drop I ever witnessed. Without any further delay the flight headed for the deck again and turned homeward. Along the route we noticed scattered flashes that may or may not have been shots directed at is. No enemy aircraft was seen at any time and no organised anti-aircraft fire was encountered.

Marked with a white recognition stripe, C-47 41-19473 was photographed at Algiers airport delivering wounded troops that it had picked up at forward airstrips along the Tunisian front. Accepted by the USAAF on 9 December 1942, this aircraft was sent to North Africa on 1 January 1943. It was eventually salvaged for parts in Italy in May 1944 (*National Archives*)

'Seconds before we reached Thelpete on the return flight, the airfield was visited by a flight of enemy aircraft, so we added to their fright some on our return. After a recognition flare, a few smudge pots were lit on the ground and we landed in vee formation, Col Lee guiding us with his landing lights. We touched down almost to the minutes, some two hours after take-off, having covered a total of 286 air miles.'

Used for intratheatre transport, this ATC C-47 overflies the Pyramids in 1943-44. Note that the aircraft retains the RAF-style fin flash, but without the usual two- or three-digit number as seen on most MTO-based C-47s (*National Archives*)

An ATC C-47 is refuelled by local personnel at Salala, Arabia, in June 1943. Such fields linked the MTO with the CBI (*National Archives*)

In December, the Troop Carrier Groups that had been in *Torch* were made part of the 51st TCW under the command of the Northwest Africa Air Forces (NAAF) (later renamed Twelfth Air Force). An average of 140 C-47 types (20-25 per cent were C-53s) were operating in the theatre in the winter of 1942-43. Intratheatre transport, casualty evacuation and delivery of mail was crucial, as was logistic support to Allied air units operating from forward airstrips, especially once the winter rains had turned roads into quagmires. This made air evacuation of the wounded from forward airfields to base hospitals in Algeria an important mission for C-47 units. An air evacuation system was put in place by mid-January.

When the German victory at Kasserine Pass threatened to overrun forward Allied airfields, these were evacuated by C-47s. When the Germans withdrew, C-47s flew in with engineers to re-open the airfields.

On 16 January 1943, Sgt Theodore Schafer of the 60th TCG was put in charge of the first 36-man medical detachment formed to fly on C-47s during casualty evacuation missions. He recalled;

'This group of men was sent up to forward bases, and after only one week of special training they began, on 26 January 1943, their missions. These missions led us into the rim of enemy held territory. Thirty-six men, all volunteers, subjected themselves to all possible hazards, flying all day long, in all types of weather and in an unarmed ship with only meagre escort on most missions. We were subjected to the strafing and bombing of enemy aeroplanes as we waited to transport the wounded from these forward fields. Sometimes this took as long as three days. Our unarmed transport aeroplanes evaded fighters sometimes by a matter of minutes.

'We were given the discretionary powers of being both doctors and nurses, as at the time only medical department enlisted personnel were available to accompany the casualties in flight. We administered morphine, redressed gaping wounds and readministered medication as the aeroplane flew through the mountains in evasive action. One of the men improvised an oxygen tent at about 10,000 ft, which probably saved the life of one wounded man. At this time there was no such thing as an evacuation station so we ate and slept where we could. Cold C rations was a delicacy, and a good many times we went without meals.'

This represented the first step in what was to become the extensive casualty evacuation infrastructure that was to emerge in the ETO/MTO. As much as the aircrew, nurses and technicians were part of the mission.

The C-47 that ended the war in North Africa. On 12 May 1943, the *SHANGRI-LA EXPRESS* flew the captured Axis high command from Tunisia to Maison Blanche airport, in Algeria (*National Archives*)

REINFORCEMENTS

Increased C-47 production (100 per month) allowed further aircraft to be sent to the MTO in the spring of 1943, although this required cutting back stateside training. The three groups of the 52nd TCW arrived in North Africa, the 61st from Britain and the 313th and 314th from the US. They were reinforced by the 316th, leaving Egypt for Algeria.

New air routes opened and the ATC European Wing was established in January 1943, soon under the command of Brig Gen Paul E Burrows (later succeeded in 1944-45 by Brig Gen Earl S Hoag). Flying C-47/53s (with a few C-48s and other impressed DC-3s), its missions included medical evacuation. In addition to an infrastructure of bases, navigation aids, and hospitals for evacuees, the ATC built its own search and rescue capability, with C-47s being used to fly in with repair crews or to evacuate survivors in the event of forced landings. The ATC opened services from Accra to Marrakech in January 1943 – the southern transatlantic route could now be extended to Britain, with a stop in Morocco en route from West Africa. In June 1943 the ATC split its Africa-Middle East Wing into the Central Africa and Middle East wings.

ATC services now stretched across North Africa. This led to the formation, in May 1943, of the Mediterranean Air Transport Service (MATS), which was a joint US-British operation (with French participation) providing air transport throughout the MTO until 1945. While most of its C-47s were assigned to ATC, it later had operational control of some 51st TCW units too.

C-47s (mostly from ATC) dominate the flightline at Waller Field, Trinidad, in 1944. Their number reveals the importance of the aircraft to the southern route between the US and the ETO/MTO. The C-47 remained vital to the intertheatre transport mission even after increased numbers of C-54s became available from early 1944 onward (*National Archives*)

MTO 1943-44

The Casablanca conference in January 1943 saw senior officer identify Sicily as the next Allied objective after Tunisia. Following the surrender of Axis forces in Tunisia in May 1943, the US 82nd and British 1st Airborne Divisions, USAAF C-47s and a small force of RAF transports provided an airborne invasion capability. NAAF/XII TCC (Provisional) was formed as headquarters for the multi-wing force, commanded by Brig Gen Paul Williams, formerly of the 51st TCW.

Sicily was heavily defended, so the airborne assault would have to be carried out at night. No one had conducted large-scale night airborne operations before, and the Troop Carrier Groups lacked pre-war doctrine to provide high level guidance. Their leaders' and cadres' experience was in the very different transport mission. The RAF, which had little combat experience with troop carriers, but had conducted considerable night operations, thought the tactics of the Troop Carrier Groups were seriously flawed. US C-47 troop carrier tactics were for each serial (of at least squadron strength) to maintain tight formation at night. Night navigation and formation flying training was seen as inadequate, especially in the 52nd TCW. Maj Gen Matthew Ridgway, leading the 82nd Airborne, requested that the airborne operations be limited to daylight. His recommendations were not approved.

With only the experience of the few battalion-size airdrops in North Africa to provide guidance, C-47 training began in June 1943. Every Troop Carrier Group C-47 in the MTO was committed to the intensive training required for airborne operations. Col Ray Dunn's 51st TCW had deployed without glider-towing training, and had little time to prepare. Their C-47s were modified to accommodate the British 1st Airborne Division's parachutes and equipment, which differed from that used by their US counterparts with which the wing had trained. While the 51st trained with the

Paul Williams – shown here as a major general in 1945, wearing IX Troop Carrier Command/First Allied Airborne Army insignia – was a key figure in determining how C-47s would be used in the ETO/MTO. Commanding, in turn, the 51st TCW, XII TCC and IX TCC, he provided a degree of continuity in command for the troop carriers that was vital in the absence of pre-war doctrine. A competent commander and a thoughtful airman, his record has been overshadowed by those associated with fighter and bomber commands in the ETO and MTO (*National Archives*)

MATS C-47 41-7763 is seen being unloaded at Gibraltar in early 1943, the aircraft still wearing a yellow-surround *Torch* insignia. Delivered to the USAAF on 28 March 1942, this aircraft was assigned to the Eighth Air Force on 2 June. It was then sent out to the Twelfth Air Force later that year, and remained in service with MATS in the MTO until withdrawn from use on 1 October 1944. MATS was not large enough in size to handle the intratheatre coordination and supply of Allied forces massing along the Mediterranean littoral prior to the invasion of Sicily (*National Archives*)

An engine is loaded aboard a C-47 'somewhere in the MTO' in the spring of 1943. One of the most important transport missions flown by the C-47 was the support of Allied air power throughout the MTO, including the airlifting of engines and repair teams to aircraft stuck on forward airfields (*National Archives*)

A C-47 of the 51st TCW takes British Glider Pilot Regiment aircrew on a training flight in a CG-4A in Algeria in June 1943. The British glider pilots found the CG-4A disturbingly fragile compared to their more familiar Airspeed Horsa (*National Archives*)

British, the 52nd TCW trained with the 82nd Airborne.

Intratheatre transport missions required to support Allied air forces came to a halt, as two squadrons of the 315th TCG had to fly down from England, having been assigned to the Twelfth Air Force AFSC.

1Lt Thomas P Dickey of the 60th TCG was already in North Africa, having flown C-47 41-38701 on the first intratheatre transport mission to Malta from Algeria on 14 April 1943. His crew consisted of 2Lt Leonard Jackley (co-pilot), 1Lt Jack Abrams (navigator), TSgt W C Thompson (engineer) and PFC Petranck (radio operator). Dickey noted;

'Departed Relizane 0700 hrs on 14 April 1943 and flew to Maison Blanche. Received a load of personnel and freight to be taken to Malta from the British Air Movements Section. Departed Maison Blanche for Tripoli at 0940 hrs, arriving at Castel Benito airfield, Tripoli, at 1430 hrs. At 1545 hrs departed Castel Benito and flew direct to Luqa airfield, Malta, arriving at 1745 hrs.

'Weather over whole route was fine except for slight frontal action between Maison Blanche and Biskra. Visibility over land was restricted due to sand haze caused by moderately high winds.

'The route flown is the most direct one between Algiers and Tripoli without climbing high enough to clear the mountains and fly a straight line. The route is Maison Blanche-Biskra-Medine-Castel Benito. No landing between Maison Blanche and Castel Benito.

'Malta has a homing station on the south coast which makes the flight relatively easy, using radio compass. An escort of one Beaufighter was provided for the flight from Tripoli to Malta. The reason for this was not explained, but such action is not the custom, since most flights to Malta are made unescorted.

'We returned to our home station the following day over the same route. No enemy aircraft was sighted or any action encountered.'

The British plan for the invasion of Sicily required a night glider assault to seize a vital bridge behind the invasion beaches. With little time to deploy their own gliders, British glider pilots were hastily sent to North Africa to be trained on CG-4As. They had not been trained in night operations. But the CG-4A gliders were late arriving in-theatre, many without their pilots, cutting back on C-47 training time. There were a number of practice missions flown, but no night glider exercises or rehearsal of the planned mass night over-water glider towing and release. In the days before the invasion, the Troop Carrier Groups and the two airborne divisions were crowded at airfields in Tunisia, distant from the planners at Allied headquarters scattered from Morocco to Cairo and the invasion force on ships throughout the Mediterranean.

OPERATION *LADBROKE*

On the night of 9-10 July, Operation *Ladbroke* was mounted from airfields in Tunisia, near Endifiaville – 105 C-47s from the 51st TCW (plus 28 RAF Albemarles and seven Halifaxes) towed 137 largely British-crewed CG-4As and eight Horsas carrying glider troops of the British 1st Airborne Division to landing zones near Syracusa. The mass take-offs led to brown-out conditions on the airfields, increasing the interval between aircraft. As the C-47 formations were directed up the narrow corridor between naval task forces, they started to become intermingled as a result of unexpected high winds aloft. Radio silence – ordered for all missions – prevented reorganisation. Other C-47s had to take evasive action to avoid potential mid-air collisions, while a quarter to a third of the intercom connections between C-47s and gliders failed.

Paratroopers of the 82nd Airborne smile for the camera inside a C-47 on their way to a practice jump prior to the invasion of Sicily (*National Archives*)

The gliders were to have been released some 3000 yards offshore, relying on their 1400-1800 ft altitude and the 15-1 glide angle of a loaded CG-4A. But with only a low half-moon, the release point was difficult to judge. Many lost C-47s released their gliders too far offshore, while others were diverted by ground fire. Some, allowing for the high winds, released their gliders at 3000 ft or higher, and a number of glider pilots released themselves.

About 80 gliders ditched, with the loss of over 250 men, and one was shot down. Only 54 gliders made it to land, 12 of them – some damaged by flak – near their LZs. A few glider troops landed near the key objective, the Ponte Grande bridge outside the city, and they were able to hold it long enough (before being surrounded and overrun) to prevent the Germans from demolishing it. The bridge was re-taken by Allied ground troops the next day. There were no losses among the transport aircraft.

OPERATION *HUSKY I*

At the other end of Sicily, while *Ladbroke* was still in progress, the 82nd Airborne arrived in the first minutes of 10 July. Some 226 C-47s of Col Hal Clark's 52nd TCW (the veteran Ninth Air Force 316th TCG attached) carried Col Jim Gavin and 2700 men of the 82nd Airborne to a DZ at Gela-Farello airfield, with the mission of seizing and holding a vital road junction east of Gela. Even though the 52nd had been thoroughly trained in glider towing stateside, its C-47s were instead loaded down with supplies in 891 parapacks (externally mounted parachute cargo bundles).

The formation, flying in serials made up of nine-ship vee-of-vees squadron formations flying in trail, cruised at 1000 ft to come in under German radar, following B-17s with radar jammers already positioned off the coast. Due to take-off delays on the airfields and unexpected high winds and navigational difficulties, the C-47s were late. Missed checkpoints over Malta disrupted and scattered all the groups except the 64th TCG – a 51st TCW group attached to the 52nd for this mission – on the way to the DZs, which were obscured by smoke from earlier bombardments. The dogleg course around the invasion fleet brought the C-47s (most of which lacked their own navigators) over the unmarked DZs in total darkness.

While the plan had been for the C-47s to arrive over the DZ in a compact mass, it took 36 minutes for the 82nd to drop, widely scattered. The 61st TCG, leading the formation, was to drop the 3-504th PIR at DZ 'Queen' on the Niscemi-Gela road. They ended up badly dispersed over large distances, with many coming down in militarily insignificant groups. The 314th TCG intended to drop the 3-505th PIR at DZ 'Tare' three miles north of Lake Bivere, but missed the checkpoints and had to circle around. One C-47 flight, carrying I Company of the 3-505th, caught sight of the DZ, peeled off, and dropped the company accurately. The rest of the group circled for a third pass before dropping their paratroops. Enough paratroopers landed near the DZ to hold a vital bridge, but most ended up 10-15 miles away.

The 313th TCG carrying the 1-505th PIR was blown off course and the paratroopers widely scattered. The 316th TCG was carrying Col Gavin and headquarters assets, and it ended up scattering them all over southern Sicily. The 64th TCG delivered the 2-505th intact, albeit some 25 miles east of its DZ, 'Sugar'. Eight C-47s were lost to flak coming off the DZ, and a further ten damaged. Three brought their paratroopers back on board, having been unable to find a DZ.

Capt Wilfred S Reiss of the 16th TCS/64th TCG was the pilot of C-47 41-18343 *Hi Babe!* during Operation *Husky I*. His crew on the mission consisted of 1Lt William P Haynes (co-pilot), 2Lt Edward P Donegan Jr (navigator), TSgt Gaylord Swisher (engineer) and Cpl Paul Seyse (radio operator). Reiss recalled;

'Nearing the coast of Sicily, we observed hundreds of dark, bulky objects below and knew they were British and American warships and landing barges awaiting the "go" signal. Ahead and to the left, we saw what looked like a whole city burning. It was a great sight.

'All was going well until we were five minutes from out target. Suddenly, our left engine sputtered. The ship shook violently, and I thought we were in for a pack of trouble. When a transport motor conks out

A vee of 52nd TCW C-47s make a low-level pass over paratroopers of the 82nd Airborne on the DZ after a training jump at Oujda, in Morocco, on 3 June 1943 (*National Archives*)

at low altitude, it usually means curtains, but somehow or other we kept flying. Lt Haynes and Sgt Swisher turned in a fine piece of work in helping to keep the ship aloft. We stayed in formation and dropped our load. We learned later that the drop was successful.

'As we headed for home, on our left flak started coming up. A searchlight caught us twice, but we lost it at low altitude. We reached the coast, with the dragging motor, at 300 ft above the water.

'The engine quit completely at this point and we had to drop out of formation. We went down to 150 ft. The water was mighty close, and we could see the waves clearly. Finally, we managed to feather the motor and this gave us a chance to fly straight and level. The other ships passed over us, one by one. Then we were alone in the darkness, limping along.

'After 30 minutes we struggled to 1000 ft and breathed easier. 2Lt Donegan set our course and Sgt Seyse radioed air sea rescue. All the time we thought we'd have to land on the water. But we kept going and then we saw the North African coast and then our field. Landing was simple. I'd landed on one engine twice before, so I didn't worry about that.'

OPERATION *HUSKY II*

Follow-on airborne operations planned for the night of 10 July were cancelled due to the confused ground situation. In Operation *Husky II-Mackall White*, hastily planned for the night of 11 July, 144 C-47s of the reinforced 52nd TCW and 61st TCG carried 2000 troops of the 504th PIR to reinforce the 82nd. The continued presence of the invasion fleets offshore led to an order to ensure that all ships would be informed of the C-47s passing overhead and would hold their fire. Ridgway had insisted on assurances on this, but found the naval command unresponsive.

Before the C-47s arrived, the Germans launched a counterattack, coordinated with a strong air attack on the invasion fleet. Immediately after this attack, the C-47s came overhead. Many ships had not gotten the order to hold fire – all had been firing in self-defence minutes before.

The fleet opened fire at the C-47s, which were easy targets in tight formation at just 800 ft. The lit recognition lights and flare signals of the C-47s were ignored. Some aircraft carrying resupply ammunition exploded in mid-air. Others, on fire, tried to ditch to save the paratroopers. The survivors were forced to take evasive action, many C-47s diving to sea level to escape. There was little formation integrity left as the C-47s arrived over Gela-Farello airfield to encounter intense German fire. Paratroopers were scattered throughout eastern Sicily. Heading for home, the scattered C-47s encountered blacked-out ships at low altitude, leading to more losses. A total of 23 C-47s were downed, 60 badly and 39 slightly damaged – 318 paratroopers were casualties. The 316th TCG's formation was worst hit, losing 12 C-47s to naval gunfire.

It was one of the worst fratricide incidents of the war. In the words of Flt Off Homer Anderson Jr and 2Lt John W Harpster, pilot and co-pilot of a C-47 of the 45th TCS/316th TCG, 'The safest place for us tonight over Sicily would have been over enemy territory'.

OPERATION *FUSTIAN*

In Operation *Fustian*, on the night of 13 July, 105 51st TCW C-47s and 11 Albemarles carried British paratroops to seize the vital Primasole

Groundcrew examine the wing of a C-47 at a North African base after it was damaged in the invasion of Sicily. Note that the wing insignia has the *Torch* yellow surround, this early-production aircraft also lacking any green overspray (*National Archives*)

Bridge near Catania, followed by 19 RAF gliders towed by Albemarles and Halifaxes.

Again, the flight path was overhead the invasion fleet. This time, the ships did get the word that the C-47s were coming, but while the transports were over the British ships, German bombers appeared. It was a repeat of the previous massacre. Even when the cease-fire order was passed by radio, naval gunners on merchant ships did not get the word. Friendly fire claimed 11 C-47s, with the enemy accounting for a further three. Fifty more were damaged.

The C-47s were badly scattered and lost, following evasive action – 27 returned without delivering their loads. Only four gliders made it to the LZ, yet despite this, the few British paratroopers that landed seized and held the bridge.

1Lt Lee D Carr of the 10th TCS/60th TCG was pilot of C-47 42-23481 during Operation *Fustian*. His crew consisted of 2Lt Wilfred Buersmeyer (co-pilot), SSgt John H Wallace (crew-chief/aerial engineer) and Sgt Victor A Schwartz (radio operator). The aircraft carried British paratroopers. Carr remembers;

'We passed over a convoy at a point midway between Malta and the southeast coast of Sicily and answered a challenge – no fire resulted. Minutes later we passed over another convoy east southeast of Syracuse that immediately started firing on us. We flashed the red identification under the fuselage but the firing continued, more accurate this time.

'We turned east and went further out to sea. After flying our time and distance, we headed toward shore and made a landfall south of the river leading to the drop zones. We turned north at this point and flew at sea level up the river and turned to our final run-in-heading at the first turn of the river. This was the last point at which we saw Lt Raymond Runzel, our wingman in C-47 42-68714. We also saw several large flares off to the northeast over the water.

'We began our ascent at the east end of drop zone number four and were spotted by the searchlight at 350 ft. We had a large volume of light and heavy flak concentrated on the ship at this point, and several hits were received. We gave the paratroopers the green light at 400 ft, but only four or five got out before our evasive action threw them to the floor. The light was on us all this time, and the fire became more accurate until we started our evasive action. It was in this, the first pass, that the small cargo door behind the pilot was shot off. A bad hit was received in the tail section.

'We turned off the green light, dropped down to tree-top level and continued on inland. We circled inland for a short time, and with excellent aid of the crew chief, radio operator and co-pilot, reorganised the paratroopers and prepared for a second run-in. We then went back and over the same drop zone at 450 ft. The searchlight picked us up again, and the fire from the north rocked the ship. Several hits were received up through the floor of the fuselage, and tracer fire was observed passing through the aircraft. Four or five more troopers got out before evasive action again threw them to the floor.

'On this second pass the crew chief was pushed out while trying to keep the static lines untangled. He had a regulation seat type parachute on, and it is not known whether he reached the remaining troopers, dropped down and headed for DZ No 3, where we saw a stick drop ahead of us.

'We noticed that the aeroplane was very sluggish, and it responded to the controls very slowly. Apparently some of the control surfaces were out of commission. The first man out over DZ No 3 was tangled in the static line of the next trooper, and as a result the 'chute of the second paratrooper was opened as he went out. The 'chute went out and hopelessly entangled the remaining five troopers, who were again thrown to the floor by evasive action.

'We again went down to tree-top level and headed for the coast. We observed one burning aeroplane on the heights south of the drop area. As we passed over the coast a searchlight and a shore battery opened up and we again attempted evasive action.

'I neglected to take into consideration the fact that the ship was not very responsive, and we hit the water, tearing off the right engine and damaging the left prop. We somehow managed to get off the water again but the aeroplane was vibrating badly and gradually settled. We hit the water tail first in a stalled attitude and stopped with no casualties.

'We abandoned the aircraft according to plan and managed to get three boats into the water before the it sank. One boat was shot-up and soon sank. We got the dinghy radio out, but decided not to use it, for we were only two miles off shore. Plans were to row the dinghy to Augusta, but the current was so strong that we made no headway. We went ashore at a rocky point eight or ten miles north of Augusta, and after deflating the boats and sorting our equipment, we headed inland.'

Carr, his crew and the remaining paratroopers eventually linked up with the invasion forces ashore and were returned to Tunisia.

AFTER SICILY

The lessons learned from Sicily would be vital for the planned invasion of Northwest Europe. Despite several near-disasters, Sicily proved that multi-division night airborne invasions could work. On the ground, even badly scattered airborne forces – less than 40 per cent of those dropped landed near their DZs – proved valuable in screening the invasion beaches and disorganising enemy defences, even if their losses were heavy. Routing clear of ships would be vital for future planning. But higher levels of command did not hear Gen Williams' judgment that that the ambitious plans depended 'entirely too much on precision'.

Changes were demanded by Washington, and these were implemented by C-47 crews and unit staffs. The paratroopers were emphatic that TCC had failed them. The USAAF command supported the Troop Carrier Groups, however, putting their faith in improved navigation aids, but the Army's confidence in these groups, and airborne divisions, had been shaken by Sicily. A board was convened under Maj Gen Joseph Swing, who had been summoned to Sicily from his position as commander of the 11th Airborne Division. It made recommendations on how division-sized airborne operations could remain viable, and strongly urged the use of pathfinders.

Some Troop Carrier Groups scheduled for deployment to the ETO were held back for extra training (at the expense of gaining experience with European weather conditions). In the US, as in the MTO, the need to use C-47s for transport missions had cut into training for the primary troop carrier mission. Excellent Troop Carrier Group and airborne

Casualty evacuation C-47s were often the first Allied aircraft into any liberated airfield, bringing in fuel and munitions for forward-deployed fighters. Here, a C-47 on a casualty evacuation mission from Sicily picks up wounded British soldiers. It carries red-bordered insignia and a chalk marking. Note also that the main cargo door hinges have been crudely reinforced 'in the field'. The gunports in the fuselage windows are also clearly visible (*National Archives*)

stateside performance before high-level observers in manoeuvres in the Carolinas in December 1943 (the 11th Airborne Division jumped and took an objective held by the 17th Airborne Division) allayed some of the fears.

OPERATIONS
GIANT I-IV

C-47 losses were replaced and training for airborne assaults re-commenced in July, leading up to full-scale night exercises (including naval involvement) by the end of August. Both TCC and the 82nd Airborne trained pathfinder units, each Troop Carrier Group forming a pathfinder flight of three C-47s. They would precede the main formation by 30 minutes to drop the 82nd's Pathfinders. On landing, they would mark the DZs with lights and gasoline-soaked t-markers.

New radio navigation aids such as the 5G radio direction finding beacons, AN/APN-2 Rebecca receivers and AN/PPN-1 Eureka transmitters also arrived. The 5G radio beacon, which was first used in Italy, was a British portable AM radio with a 40-mile range that could be received by the C-47's radio compass. Much reliance was placed on the Rebecca/Eureka system of tactical radio navigation, first used in North Africa. The C-47's Rebecca interrogated the hand-held Eureka on the ground, which responded with a coded signal.

TCC trained throughout August in Tunisia. At this time the Ninth Air Force headquarters moved to England, leaving behind the 316th TCG. TCC then moved to Sicilian airfields, along with the 82nd Airborne Division, on 2 September, ready to jump into Italy.

Operation *Giant II* would have used 135 C-47s for a planned direct air landing at five airfields around Rome, joining with the Italian garrison against their German occupiers. This was ultimately rejected, due largely to a lack of confidence in the new Italian allies, but the problems of inserting and sustaining forces by air as demonstrated in Sicily also played a part in the final decision not to jump. Covert negotiations in Rome by Brig Gen Maxwell Taylor (then artillery commander of the 82nd Airborne) and Col William Gardiner (intelligence staff officer A-2 of the 51st TCW) persuaded Gen Eisenhower to scrap *Giant II* on 6 September. The cancellation order came at 1730 hrs, with 42 gliders hooked up and US paratroopers in 93 C-47s waiting for take-off at 1830 hrs.

TCC and the 82nd, prepared for *Giant II*, were unavailable for a comparable role at H-Hour in Operation *Avalanche* – the invasion of Italy at Salerno at dawn on 9 September. Prior to *Giant II* taking out the airborne forces from *Avalanche*, plans had been drafted for paratroopers to either block key mountain passes or, alternatively, the Volturno River crossings (Operations *Giant I*), thus preventing German reinforcements from attacking the beachhead. Either option, to be mounted on 9 September, would have committed the airborne forces to sustained defensive battles without reinforcement, and required unescorted resupply missions by C-47s.

The night paratroop drop at Salerno on 13 September was not part of the original *Avalanche* plan. Rather, Lt Gen Mark Clark, the US Army commander at Salerno, requested it early on 13 September in an effort to rapidly insert reinforcements after the Germans counterattacked. Unlike Sicily, the paratroops would be dropped over friendly territory at Paestum on the River Sele, the southern flank of the beachhead.

C-47s of the 52nd TCW were already standing ready to drop two battalions of the 504th PIR on the Volturno crossing at Capua that night in an operation designated Operation *Giant I* (Revised). But after Lt Gen Clark sent a map with the new DZ marked hand-carried by a fighter pilot from a forward airstrip to Sicily, a quick message to NAAF HQ approved the decision to cancel the Capua drop and respond to Clark's request.

A Jeep from the 82nd Airborne's 80th Anti-Tank and Anti-Aircraft battalion is loaded into a C-47 for air transport. The aircraft's ability to lift such cargo internally was key to air mobility, but it could not airdrop vehicles or artillery pieces, which had to be delivered by glider. This reflected the C-47's airliner origins. Designed-for-purpose troop carrier aircraft, in production by 1945, were able to airdrop such loads, however (*Author's Collection*)

The response by the TCC and the 82nd, standing by on Sicily, was near instantaneous. Planning started at 1540 hrs on 13 September. The staffs, concerned about friendly fire, extracted a guarantee that all Allied anti-aircraft, ashore and afloat, would hold their fire after 2100 hrs that night. Mission orders were issued at 1930 hrs. The 313th TCG would fly from Trapani, while at Comiso airfield, where the 61st and 314th TCGs were loading paratroopers, a hasty outdoor briefing was held. The mission map was taped up on the side of a C-47 fuselage as the aircraft were loaded for Operation *Giant I/II* (revised). No one had time to agree on a codename.

Eight pathfinder C-47s, carrying the 82nd Airborne Pathfinder Company took off at 2045 hrs, followed by the main formation of 82 C-47s, carrying 1300 men of the 504th PIR. Despite bright moonlight and calm air, it was hard to keep the hastily planned formations together. The pathfinder C-47s delivered their paratroopers directly to the DZ, south of the River Sele, which they quickly marked with the aid of engineers that had been waiting for them. While the main formation took several hours longer than planned to come over the DZ, it delivered the paratroopers as an organised fighting unit. No aircraft were lost.

On the night of 14-15 September, Operation *Giant IV* – a follow-up drop by 125 C-47s with the 505th PIR – was also successful. Described as 'most urgent', it was ordered at 1340 hrs on the 14th. Like its predecessor, its DZ at Sele was behind Allied lines. The same planning – including the air defence 'guns tight' notification – was repeated from the previous night. As with *Giant I/II* (revised), the coordination of the formations broke down, but the weather conditions and the absence of opposition prevented this from becoming a problem. The pathfinders again worked effectively, with almost all the 1900 paratroopers landing within 200 yards of the DZ. *Giant V*, a 98-glider reinforcement mission, was cancelled as unneeded.

Concurrent with *Giant IV*, *Giant III* was carried out by 40 C-47s of the 64th TCG, dropping 640 men of the 2-509th PIR and airborne engineers near Avellino, some 15

XII TCC C-47s practice formation flying off Sicily for Operation *Giant*. Such training always competed with the requirement for C-47s to service intratheatre transport routes (*National Archives*)

miles behind German lines in mountainous terrain. The paratroopers were to use charges to block all routes through the area. There were no suitable DZs near the objectives.

Pathfinder C-47s delivered the 82nd's pathfinders to the wrong DZ. Despite this, they considered the DZ adequate, and marked it with a 5G transmitter and lights – the 64th TCG had not received Rebecca. This contributed to navigational confusion.

Most C-47s were cruising at 4300 ft, looking for the marked DZs, before descending carefully to 700 ft to drop. Many were unable to find the DZ. The formation broke apart into three squadron serials.

The need to drop from 1500-2500 ft above ground level due to the mountainous terrain resulted in the paratroops being further scattered. One squadron missed the initial point (IP) where it had to turn to the original DZ. It had to circle back to the coast and make a new approach. The other two squadrons dropped their paratroopers up to 12 miles from the planned DZ. Only 15 C-47s dropped within five miles of the DZ.

All the C-47s returned to base. The paratroopers, suffering over 20 per cent losses, destroyed a key bridge, but otherwise the operation had little effect. The problems with carrying out night paratroop drops were not resolved, and the feasibility of flying tight formations at night without navigators on most C-47s remained unchallenged.

Capt Richard Lawrence of the 64th TCG flew as co-pilot on C-47 41-18341 *Lady from Hades*, which was the lead ship following the pathfinder on Operation *Giant III*. The aircraft's crew comprised Lt Col John Cerny (pilot, and 64th TCG CO), 1Lt John Stewart (navigator), 1Lt Harry T Fontaine (intelligence observer), SSgt Edwin Nelson (crew chief) and Sgt James Dowd (radio operator).

Paratroopers of Stick No 1 included Lt Col Doyle Yardley, CO of the 2-509th PIR, who was captured after landing. Capt Lawrence related after the mission;

'We were airborne at 2135 hrs, with a full moon lighting our way. Every ship was airborne within 19$\frac{1}{2}$ minutes. Fifteen minutes before Stick No 1 took off, Capt Lively had lifted his *Birmingham Special* – the pathfinder aircraft – into the air and was now well on course.

'The flight was uneventful until we neared Salerno. About 25 miles out, Col John motioned ahead. Near the shoreline and back in the hills we could see cannon bursts, and it was concluded that an artillery duel was petering out. The flashes were not frequent, rather intermittent. This tied in with the story told later by Capt Lively, who reported that when he approached the coast, a "hot" artillery duel was going on, with bomb and cannon bursts incessant, and flares bursting as high as 3000 ft.

'At 2000 ft we saw the river south of Salerno, made our turn and started to climb. If we were to get any flak, we would get it now, but as the seconds ticked away, nothing happened. The distant flares and bomb bursts were just colourful decorations, and made no one uneasy. Then we saw the gorge.

'*Lady from Hades* nosed up to 4300 ft and cleared the first ridge. We were high over a narrow gorge, the peaks of which seemed to brush the wing tips. Off to the left we saw ground fires, probably the result of the afternoon's visit of our bombers. Far below, limestone roads stood out in white brightness. We proceeded, and we learned later that the others did, too, for about two minutes before discovering that we were in the wrong gorge, so similar were these wonders of nature. Casually, as one would hop over a slit trench, Col John pulled up the *Lady* 100 ft and did a 90-degree turn through a creak in the ridge on our left.

'"This is it", he said, and came down slowly to about 4000 ft. We continued the course, hugging the side of the gorge. Col John's guess that there would be few, if any, enemy installations in the mountains proved true. Fortunately, not a shot was fired at us.

'Presently, and directly ahead, in the area of our DZ, we saw red flashings. Up to this tine, although we recognised many of the landmarks, we had received nothing on the radio. But the red flashings, then very distinctly the red "N" by Aldis lamp, confirmed our position.

'On, or about, this time Lt Col Yardley was talking with our intelligence observer from his post on No 1 seat in the aeroplane. "You know", he said, "I feel fine about this jump. I feel that I have a horseshoe in my pocket".

'But the red warning light came on. The paratroopers sprang to readiness. All hooked up without confusion and then the green light and Col Yardley's yell, "Let's go"! The aeroplane was cleared in split seconds. The time was 13 seconds after midnight.

'Normally, we dropped paratroopers between 700 and 900 ft, but the drop this night was long, very long – 1500 ft, due to the mountainous terrain. If the element of surprise was not with the boys of the 509th, it was likely there would be casualties before they hit the ground.

'As the last man left the ship, Col John made a 170-degree climbing turn and started the run home. The problem now was to steer clear of heavy flak. To avoid Jerry's fire, we hugged the side of the gorge, keeping well below the jagged peaks. Ground fires – more than when we entered the gorge – blazed brightly. To the right, and apparently from our ships in Salerno harbour, cannon bursts were seen. Away to our left behind the mountains, artillery flashes from the German lines were visible. Shortly, we reached the coast and made the final turn for Comiso airfield.

'On the beach at Salerno there was great activity. The DZ of the 61st (for Operation *Giant IV*) was clearly visible. As we approached the area, we were challenged. Col John quickly flashed our recognition lights. The rest of the flight to our base was uneventful.'

C-47s IN THE MTO

C-47s, following the Salerno invasion, airdropped supplies. On 17 September, 24 62nd TCG aircraft made an emergency airlift of artillery shells, and the following day 50 C-47s airlifted in the 82nd Airborne's divisional headquarters. Transports also flew resupply missions to the first fighter units in Italy and, using forward airstrips, evacuated wounded. With the capture of bases on the Foggia plain, the US Fifteenth Air Force and the RAF's No 205 Group established a southern front for the combined Allied bomber offensive. This required additional intratheatre transport support, linking the hastily improvised (and often mud-choked) Italian bases with England and North Africa.

Using Italian bases, C-47s were soon dropping supplies to partisans in Italy and the Balkans. Troop Carrier Group crews also became experienced in special operations, and in October 1943 supplies were dropped to Allied PoWs evading German troops in northern Italy. Other supply drops were made to resupply advancing Allied troops.

Lt Col Raymond A Nowotny, commanding officer of the 8th TCS, personally flew many of the squadron's most dangerous special operations missions in the winter of 1943-44, and was duly awarded the Distinguished Flying Cross for his efforts.

The official report written by Nowotny for Operation *Hotspot Substitute* – an airdrop to Italian partisans harbouring Allied PoWs – indicates the dangers facing C-47 crews flying special operations (and also the close integration with the RAF that characterised the employment of the C-47 in this theatre);

'This report is submitted in response to a request for details concerning *Hotspot* mission. The originally scheduled mission was postponed, and another substituted in its place involving similar reasons.

'Mission was carried out on the night of 8/9 December 1943. One aircraft – C-47 42-118681 – was used. Crew consisted of Lt Col R A Nowotny (pilot), Capt J J McNeill (co-pilot), Lt J Piatak (navigator), TSgt R A Holmes (crew chief) and Sgt E H Chapman (radio operator). In addition to the aircrew, the British provided four enlisted men as a crew to perform necessary duties before and during flight.

'The aircraft was loaded with 12 panniers containing boots, clothing, blankets, medical supplies, food and maps. Loading was accomplished by experienced British crew. Rollers were installed to facilitate evacuation of the panniers. In addition, one container was attached to a para-rack. This container held equipment for the British crew, and was to be released only in case of necessity for bailing out.

An interior view of a C-47 on a parachute supply drop mission over Italy in 1944. On a signal from the flight crew, the 'pusher' and the 'kicker' would manhandle bundles out the door. The C-47's crew was often reinforced for this task, using volunteer groundcrew, personnel from Quartermaster Corps units or, in the MTO, British soldiers or airmen. The time taken to manually drop multiple bundles often required multiple passes over a DZ to deliver a load, increasing C-47 vulnerability. This led to conveyor devices being used, starting with the invasion of southern France, but these proved vulnerable to jamming under combat conditions (*National Archives*)

C-47s sit surrounded by great pools of water on the ground at Brindisi in the early spring of 1944. Wet conditions hampered air operations in Italy for much of the year, making C-47s invaluable for moving priority cargo and performing casualty evacuation when the roads became quagmires and the rail service was disrupted by the effects of Allied bombing (*National Archives*)

'Preparations for the mission included study of routes, weather and maps in co-operation with Sqn Ldr Dennis, Advance "N" Section, and Gp Capt Horgan of (MA)TAF. Information obtained concerned our own gun-defended positions at San Savero, Lucera and Sangro River Valley, as well as enemy positions to be avoided at coastal points, particularly Giulianova, San Benedetto and Porto Civitanova.

Alternate landing fields were indicated as Foggia Nos 1 and 2, Capaccio, Paestum, and Grottaglie. Use of Bari and Brindisi were discouraged. Altitude out was recommended at 2000-3000 ft up to Brigit Islands, and 5000 ft thereafter.

'Maps used were 1:500,000 Naples and 1/250,000 Italy, sheets San Severo, Chieti and Ancona. The route planned was as follows – Gioia, Foggia, Trimiti Islands, Pedaso and the DZ at Monte Giorgio, returning thence in similar manner.

'A final weather report was obtained at 2000 hrs local time from TAF Met Station at San Spirito. The forecast indicated visibility fair, and high cloud cover. Moonrise at 1454 hrs and moonset at 0331 hrs (9 December). Winds at 5000 ft given as 260 degrees at 25 mph, and at 2000 ft, 250 degrees at 15-20 mph, unreliable, and surface winds west-southwest, light variable.

'Take-off was planned for 2100 hrs. This was not possible due to heavy ground fog limiting visibility to 50 yards. Take-off was made at 2324 hrs under instrument conditions due to prevailing ground fog. Departed the field at 2334 hrs at 3000 ft. Overhead Foggia at 0022 hrs, Caprara passed at 0031 hrs, then turned and hit coast of Italy again 15 miles south of Pedaso at 0106 hrs.

'Proceeded northward along the coast, seeking orientation. Made run-in at Pedaso to vicinity of Monte Giorgio. Unable to definitely established position due to a great number of rivers and trails of similar appearance. Headed back towards coast and picked up cape south of Ancona. Then flew southward along coast to river valley north of Fermo. Made run into DZ from east to west at about 3500 ft, surveying terrain. Altitude of DZ about 1500 ft. Made 180-degree turn and dropped panniers just east of town of Monte Giorgio at 0141 hrs.

'Continued on 100-degree heading to dead reckoning point 24 miles off coast at Pedaso. Were able to definitely identify Pedaso, and Fermo on run out. Turned at DR point at 0154 hrs. At 0215 hrs, radio operator in navigator's dome reported unidentified aircraft at "six o'clock" position. It dove off to right and under our aircraft and was not sighted again.

'Arrived Lake Lesina 0232 hrs, from where beacon flashing at Foggia No 2 (of which we were previously informed) could be seen. Arrived Foggia No 2 at 0244 hrs. Field lights were on. Unable to contact Foggia Main. Landing made at Foggia No 2 at 0300 hrs. Landing made there because of waning moon, and lack of information concerning weather conditions at Gioia.

'No flak encountered throughout flight.

'On morning of 9 December, while crew was asleep in aircraft, a Baltimore ran its engines up within about 20 ft of the tail surfaces of our aircraft. The air stream caused thereby damaged elevator locks, elevators and two instruments on our aircraft. Later, four crew members returned via another aircraft to Gioia, arriving there at 1515 hrs on 9 December. One crew member (crew chief) was left with our aircraft to supervise repairs.

'During flight, a beacon at home field remained available, for homing purposes. Operators were standing by on command sets on ground since tower was inoperative.

'Wind forecast for 3000 ft accurate up to Trimiti Islands. Winds for 5000 ft inaccurately forecast. Report of navigator is to effect that there were very light winds from west. Vertical visibility after take-off, good.

'British crew reports 12 panniers evacuated in 20 seconds. Panniers released about 1500 ft above terrain.

'It is recommended that the time for pushing out panniers can be cut considerably by flying with tail low at time of evacuation, since this permits panniers to be rolled "downhill" to the door. This is important to note because most pilots who have dropped troops have become accustomed to flying with tail high. It is also recommended that whenever possible, signals should be used to identify drop areas. This is especially recommended in areas where the terrain is difficult to identify.'

On the night of 12 January 1944, Nowotny flew a C-47 that successfully airdropped a British 2nd Special Air Service Regiment team for Operation *Pomegranate* – a direct attack on a German airfield that was being used against the Anzio beachhead. Nowotny's C-47 – the same aeroplane as flown on the previous mission – did not return from the airdrop. He had on board the same crew, but with Sgt S Singer serving as radio operator, and with flight surgeon Capt J L Nocentini along for the experience. RAF Wellingtons flying a diversionary mission reported encountering severe icing in the area where the C-47 was lost.

ANZIO

In January 1944, training started for Operation *Sun Assault*, which was to be the airborne component of Operation *Shingle*, the Anzio invasion. *Sun Assault's* aim was to use 178 C-47s of the 52nd TCW (including nine new radar-equipped lead ships) to drop the 504th PIR (reinforced) near Anzio, staging from bases near Naples. Just 48 hours before launching, the mission was cancelled and the paratroopers – plus a British airborne brigade – were sent to Anzio by sea instead. C-47s were used to try and keep the beachhead's airstrip resupplied and operational.

Logistics difficulties, bombed ports and railway lines and roads turned into swamps made the air transportation of priority cargo and personnel vital in the first winter of the Italian campaign.

With the disbandment of XII TCC, control of the the 51st TCW passed to the Mediterranean Allied Tactical Air Force (MATAF). The British 1st and US 82nd Airborne Divisions returned to England to prepare for the invasion of Northwest Europe, followed by the 52nd TCW. Finally, the 64th TCG, 4th TCS and a number of ATC C-47s left Italy for an emergency deployment to the CBI theatre in April, 1944.

D-DAY

The build-up of forces in Britain for the June 1944 invasion of France, codenamed Operation *Overlord*, was supported by transatlantic flights by both the ATC and NATS. The Joint Army Navy Air Transport Committee, set up under the Joint Chiefs of Staff, coordinated the operation.

The ATC had by then been expanded with military aircrew, leaving airlines to operate just a quarter of the 1944 air cargo effort, compared to 87 per cent in 1942. The C-47s of ATC's European Wing, flying intratheatre missions in all weathers, were almost all flown by USAAF aircrew. Increasing numbers of four-engined aircraft (C-54/R5Ds) flew the northern transatlantic route, using the Azores as a base.

NATS reinforced VR-1 with R5Ds for the north Atlantic run, keeping its R4Ds to support bases in Iceland and Newfoundland. NATS established VR-7 to fly R4Ds on south Atlantic routes.

As a perfect example of a VIP transport mission on the North Atlantic run, the actress Marlene Dietrich, on her way to entertain troops in the ETO, stops in Iceland. She is posing with Maj Walter Slifer, pilot of the C-47 *We Don't Monkey*, and Iceland-based senior officers (*National Archives*)

ATC European Wing intratheatre transport had to be supplemented by Troop Carrier Groups, often creating conflicts with training for airborne missions. ATC C-47s met each C-54 arriving in Britain, delivering passengers and cargo to their ultimate destination.

The 27th TG, which was part of the Eighth Air Force, and later operationally subordinate to US Strategic Air Forces (USSTAF), provided intratheatre transport. The Ninth Air Force – in England since October 1943 – had its own 31st TG. These groups lacked the Troop Carrier Group's airdrop and glider tow

A NATS R4D circles over Sugar Loaf Mountain near Rio de Janeiro in 1943. The substantial US Navy air presence in Brazil during the Battle of the Atlantic required constant airlift support from NATS (*National Archives*)

1Lt Jimmie Mah of the 27th TG poses in front of a natural metal C-47 at Prestwick in 1944. Transport Group aircraft, unlike those operated by the Troop Carrier Groups, were not usually fitted with Rebecca direction finding gear. A transatlantic ATC C-54 and an inbound B-24J are lined up on the flightline. Wartime censoring has deleted the background. The diminutive Mah was later killed when the B-17 he was flying from Warton to Kettering crashed en route (*Author's Collection*)

C-47 air (from the 27th TG and other outfits) and ground NCOs, based at Warton, Lancashire, pose for a photo in 1944. The author's father, TSgt Joseph Isby, is on the right (*Author's Collection*)

missions, and without the need to practice these skills, could devote all their flight hours to intratheatre transport in all weathers. Service groups and depots often had flights with one or a few C-47s attached, while US Navy units in the ETO/MTO also operated a few R4Ds.

With six independent C-47/R4D operators in the ETO/MTO, no one headquarters could coordinate and prioritise their use, so Supreme Headquarters Allied Expeditionary Forces (SHAEF) set up a Combined Air Transport Operations Room (CATOR) to coordinate the Allied resupply of the invasion (outside of the operations of airborne forces), but this was far from being a central headquarters.

Some may have repeated the Fifth Air Force jibe that ATC stood for 'allergic to combat', but the command paid a high price in men and aeroplanes to keep the transatlantic air routes to the ETO/MTO open. This ATC C-47A (42-100496) crashed at Fort Pepperdell, in Newfoundland, on 24 November 1943. The wreck is being inspected by a search party in the photograph (*National Archives*)

Most C-47s in the ETO/MTO were part of the Troop Carrier Groups. The Ninth Air Force took over the England-based 50th and 53rd TCWs, forming IX TCC in October 1943 under Brig Gen Benjamin Giles – Brig Gen Paul Williams took over in February 1944, and remained in charge until VE-Day. Originally, VIII Air Support Command (ASC) had been intended to command the TCWs, and the provisional TCC from their headquarters were used to form IX TCC. They were joined by personnel from I TCC and most of the staff of XII TCC that had flown, along with the 52nd TCW and half the 315th TCG, to England from North Africa.

Initial growth was slow (there were only 353 ETO-based C-47s in February 1944), but by March IX TCC had grown from its original six bases in East Anglia, adding five in Berkshire and Wiltshire and three in Somerset and the west. It had reached its planned strength of three TCWs (two without combat experience) commanding 14 Troop Carrier Groups (nine without combat experience). The RAF also built up its transport squadrons as more lend-lease Dakotas arrived.

Douglas Aircraft rushed a batch of 400 over-plan C-47s to completion in time for the invasion. Over 1200 IX TCC C-47s would be put into the air for the invasion, with over 800 for the initial airdrops alone. Troop Carrier Group authorised strength was increased to 64 (later, after D-Day, 80) C-47/53s and nine (later 16) spares. IX TCC groups grew to well over this size, keeping older C-47s as replacements arrived, with 80-110 aircraft common by May (five to ten per cent being C-53s). Groundcrew numbers did not expand, however, straining resources.

Troop Carrier Groups were, unlike other combat units, multi-type, including gliders, liaison aircraft and, often, a few C-87s or C-109s (converted B-24s). As groups were often sent into battle usually without a veteran cadre or pre-war doctrine to provide guidance, this put a premium on unit leaders. Strong group and squadron commanders left their mark, leading from the front. Tours of duty varied, and in November 1943 they were set at 800 hours of 'green ink' (operational) flying. There was generally less personnel turnover at both cockpit and command level in the C-47 groups than within bomber units.

Individual flying experience within IX TCC was much better than it had been in 1942. Pilots were required to have at least 450 hours total flying time, and most had more, as in the 315th TCG where they averaged 1500 hours. Only the newly arrived 442nd TCG suffered from a concentration of low-hours pilots. Yet, despite this improved standard of individual training and airmanship, there was a shortage of trained crews. Each C-47 was supposed to have two crews. While some groups had up to 128 crews, in most there was barely one crew available per C-47.

Aircrew were rushed from the US to IX TCC. This meant that on D-Day, 20 per cent of C-47 aircrew committed to operations had been

Brig Gen Maurice M Beach was commander of the 53rd TCW from August 1942 through to VE-Day. While groups and squadrons were frequently commanded by reservists, wing-level and higher command remained in the hands of pre-war Air Corps officers such as Beach. Wing-level planning and training was more important for Troop Carrier Groups than ETO Bomb Groups, where it was largely administrative in nature (*National Archives*)

A 91st TCS C-47 crew practices the 'pick-up' method of towing a glider into the air at Upottery in May 1944. Although tricky, crews soon mastered this form of snatch technique, and used it to great effect in the ETO (*National Archives via Roger Freeman*)

overseas for less than 60 days – insufficient time to train for European weather and operational conditions, however many flight hours they had previously logged. In many groups, only one C-47 in three had a navigator. But troop carrier tactics depended on C-47s being able to keep together in tight serial formations at night.

A nine-ship 'vee of vees' from the 437th TCG drops paratroopers over the DZ near Ramsbury in January 1944. Were they dropping supplies, they would be lower than the 500 ft altitude seen here (*National Archives*)

Training intensified throughout the winter and spring of 1944, shifting to joint troop carrier-airborne forces training starting on 15 March. Besides building up the unit skills needed, staffs and aircrew alike worked on ways to avoid the failures of Sicily. Maj Gen Matthew Ridgway, commanding the 82nd Airborne, had asked, as a vote of confidence, that the 52nd TCW and his division become permanently linked, with their only duties being training with the 82nd, or carrying it into action. But C-47s were too valuable to be dedicated to any one unit. During pre-D-Day training, the groups' duties included medical evacuation of casualties from the air battles raging over Germany – C-47s flew them from base hospitals to ATC C-54s at Prestwick, bound for the US.

Early proposals by IX TCC (supported by US Army Chief of Staff Gen George B Marshall and USAAF HQ in Washington) for a deep strike invasion emphasised troop carriers – first dropping two airborne divisions to seize an airfield near Evreux, then flying in two further reinforcing divisions. These were rejected, but filed away for future use. Rather, airborne divisions would be inserted in coordination with the amphibious invasion, providing flank guards and a blocking force. The Troop Carrier Groups would provide resupply until link-up.

The extent and number of the airborne landings were in flux until almost the last minute, depending on varying projections of C-47 survivability and accuracy in delivering paratroopers and gliders. Commander of the Allied Expeditionary Air Forces (AEAF) – to which IX TCC had been made operationally subordinate in December 1943 – Air Chief Marshal Sir Trafford Leigh-Mallory emerged as a major opponent of the airborne portion of the plan. Based on RAF experience with night low-level operations, he estimated that a third to half the C-47s might be lost, and made personal appeals up the chain of command to cancel the airdrops. Indeed, substantial resistance in the planning process had to be overcome to ensure the inclusion of two US and one British airborne divisions. They would drop at night in the first hours of D-Day. Leigh-

Senior Allied officers visited a number of tactical units at bases in southern England in the weeks leading up to Operation *Neptune*. One such visit was made by Air Chief Marshal Sir Trafford Leigh-Mallory, Commander-in-Chief Allied Expeditionary Air Forces, who was an outspoken critic of the airborne portion of the D-Day plan. Here, he addresses men of the 434th TCG from the control tower at Aldermaston (*National Archives via Roger Freeman*)

Mallory set up a Combined Troop Carrier Command Post (CTCCP) to coordinate IX TCC and RAF units, but US operational units and planners tended to bypass it.

Pathfinder C-47s would precede the main force to the DZs and LZs, dropping specially trained para-troops that would mark them for the approaching main force. Pathfinder C-47s were modified with Gee, the British radio direc-tion-finding triangulation system with a margin of error of about a mile over Normandy. Pathfinder

C-47s of the 434th and 435th TCGs fly over the Horsa gliders that they have just released on the south side of Ramsbury airfield during an exercise with the 101st Airborne Division on 6 January 1944 (*National Archives via Roger Freeman*)

and lead ship C-47s carried the SCR-717C, a version of the H2X ground mapping radar used to bomb through overcasts. However, this was designed to pick up major terrain features, such as coastlines and rivers, and required radar reflectors or beacons set up on a DZ/LZ to locate it.

However, IX TCC still emphasised navigating by serial, as they had over Sicily. The USAAF lacked trained navigators for C-47s, with many groups having them only in serial or element lead ships. The RAF again urged them to adopt their tactics of navigating by individual aircraft, and emphasising Gee and pathfinders. But RAF senior navigators had flown with Bomber Command, and had learned bitter lessons on the difficulty of night navigation over occupied Europe. The RAF fitted all their Dakotas with Gee (the USAAF lacked sufficient sets, and training time), and relied on it rather than the Rebecca/Eureka that IX TCC emphasised. Every C-47 in IX TCC sprouted forward-facing Rebecca antennas under the cockpit side windows, and they could also use the 5G radio beacon.

Navigation was not all that the C-47s lacked. A proposal to fit IX TCC aircraft with self-sealing tanks and armour was turned down by 'Hap' Arnold. Only 75 C-47s had been delivered with them in 1942-43 before the weight penalty was considered excessive. Crews were instead authorised body armour and seat pads.

A testing programme in August 1943 determined that the C-47 could tow, with some difficulty, the larger British Airspeed Horsa glider. Fuel consumption was high, as the C-47 had to climb and cruise at high power settings. Soon adopted in large numbers by the USAAF through 'reverse Lend Lease', the Horsa still tended to drop its Y-tow rope in flight.

Three IX TCC-level and 38 wing-level training exercises were flown by day and night. The most extensive, Operation *Eagle*, was flown in good weather on the night of 11 May and was generally successful. However, a full-scale rehearsal of the entire airborne invasion was not possible due to the size of the Allied transport force – 2316 aircraft by D-Day. Nor were the effects of possible bad weather covered in the plans, or in briefings to the C-47 crews (although they had been included in *Eagle*).

D-DAY MISSIONS

The imminence of the invasion was announced on C-47 bases in England, first with the arrival of airborne troops in sealed bivouac areas at

IX TCC airfields, then with the appearance of black and white stripes painted overnight on all the aircraft – a lesson learned from the massacre of C-47s off Sicily in 1943. The gliders, their assembly and concentration on the group airfields having proven unexpectedly difficult were linked to tow ships.

Originally scheduled for the early morning hours of 5 June, the invasion was delayed 24 hours due to weather. When finally launched, the weather, though improved, was marginal. The initial airborne sorties were integrated with Operation *Neptune*, the naval element of *Overlord*, reflecting that the C-47s would be doing their work before H-Hour on the beaches, as well as the close cooperation aimed at preventing fratricide by the ships. To avoid alerting the defences, no weather reconnaissance flights were flown ahead of the missions. Route planning had also avoided overflying both the invasion fleet and German flak concentrations. The ultimate destination was the six US drop zones in Normandy.

Leading the invasion were 20 IX TCC Pathfinder Group C-47s, three for each of the six US DZs and two back-ups, taking off from

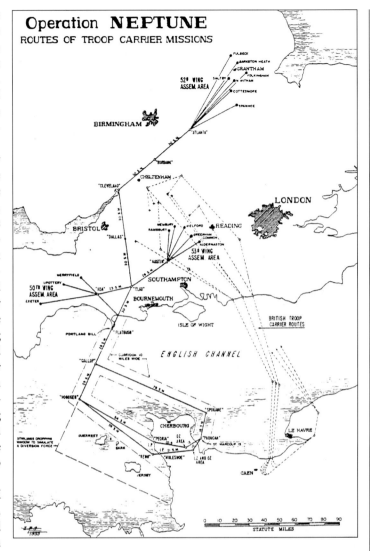

This map reveals the route taken by the various Troop Carrier Groups heading to Normandy as part of Operation *Neptune* (*Author's Collection*)

North Witham late on 5 June – 30 minutes before the main force. Bright moonlight helped navigation. Crossing the Channel at low altitude – one ditched with engine failure – the pathfinders encountered a cloud over Normandy at about 1000 ft, extending 10-12 miles inland. Some C-47s dropped below the cloud cover, drawing flak. The pathfinders navigated to the DZs by radar, Gee and dead reckoning. There was no way they could communicate with the main force about the weather, nor was there anything that could be done to compensate. No alternative plans for cloud cover had been made, despite it being a frequent condition in the Norman spring, and orders were for radio silence.

The green light went on in the first pathfinder C-47s at 0015 hrs. The pathfinder teams were only able to properly mark one of the six DZs, and the paratroopers landed within two miles of it. At another, the marker lights came on too late for the main force C-47s. The enemy was either too close or the pathfinders were unable to reach the remaining four DZs.

The main force was swiftly approaching the targets in a vast stream, pulling together C-47s from the IX TCC's 20 fields in three separated basing areas. Each wing, forming up at different times, flew at 1500 ft to navigation checkpoint 'Elko', which was marked by a radio beacon outside Blandford Forum, in Dorset. They then turned and joined the single stream of C-47s heading for Normandy. The aircraft crossed the English coast outbound over checkpoint 'Flatbush' at Portland Bill, heading southwest to avoid the invasion fleet. The massive formations were flying under the radar, descending to 1000 ft as they passed 'Flatbush', the command departure point off the English coast. The C-47s then dived to 500 ft, cruising at 140 mph without navigation or recognition lights, in total radio silence. 'Gallup', a warship with a radio beacon mid-Channel, marked the outward-bound course.

RAF Stirlings preceded the C-47s, acting as chaff bombers and providing a diversion. At point 'Hoboken', off the west coast of Normandy, the C-47s climbed to 1500 ft, turning to avoid the German-occupied Channel Islands – the flak there opened fire – and split into two parallel formations, 'Albany' to the south, 'Boston' to the north. The formations crossed the west coast of Normandy's Contentin peninsula, presenting a clear return on the radar of the lead C-47s, at 1500 ft. A main and alternate lead crew, trained at the Pathfinder School, led each serial.

After crossing the coast, the C-47s penetrated broken cloud. While descending to 500 ft for the drops, the aircraft encountered the cloud bank, now more solid between 2000 and 1000 ft. Many of the serials saw the solid cloud too late to descend under it first. The air was turbulent. Unexpected winds aloft – gusts of 30 knots following the front that had passed on 5 June – led to the formations drifting and becoming separated. This was not a contingency that had been rehearsed or briefed. But no training could keep the serial formations in the two streams together in those conditions. With each serial being a series of nine-C-47 formations flying in trail, any disruption was soon transmitted down the long stream.

Nine of the 20 serial formations of C-47s committed to 'Albany' and 'Boston' penetrated the cloud deck, and became disrupted. The wind picked up, increasing above 15 knots. The squadron formations, flying in trail, lost sight of the group lead ships with their radar and Gee for navigation. Lower altitude also reduced the range at which Rebecca could pick up Eureka. Other C-47s held on top of it, relying on Rebecca, or managed to navigate around it. Even though only

While no photographs were possible of the night drop on D-Day, this sketch by a C-47 crew member (Capt Creekmore) who was there conveys an idea of the confusion that prevailed – clouds, parachutes, gliders and formations intermingling. In reality, the paratroopers were all on the ground before the first gliders arrived (*National Archives*)

C-47s of the 440th TCG's 95th and 98th TCSs are seen at Exeter on the afternoon of 5 June 1944 following the application of their invasion stripes. With more than 60 aircraft on strength on the eve of D-Day, the group had to park a number of its C-47s on the grass, rather than on hardstandings (*National Archives via Roger Freeman*)

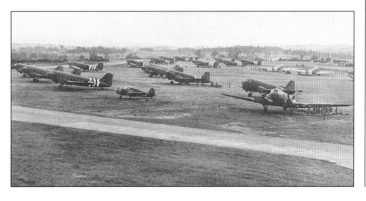

squadron leads were supposed to be using Rebecca, the multiple Eureka sets soon interfered with each other and, in rain, showed positions that were up to two miles in error.

Mission 'Albany' – 432 C-47s heading for the IP at checkpoint 'Reno', before breaking up the stream to head to the individual DZs 'Able', 'Charlie' and 'Dog' behind the exits of Utah Beach – was the 101st Airborne's drop, with two serials of the 438th TCG in the lead, followed by four serials from the 436th and 439th TCGs, followed by one each from the 435th, 441st and 440th TCGs. Of these, the later serials had better success in keeping the paratroopers together and closer to the drop zone.

Mission 'Boston's' 369 C-47s were carrying the 82nd Airborne's 6418 paratroopers. These aircraft were mainly from the 82nd's old comrades, the 52nd TCW, heading for IP 'Paducah' and then to DZs 'Nan', 'Oboe' and 'Tare', further inland around the crossings of the River Merderet and the crossroads town of Ste Mere Eglise. Two serials of the 316th TCG were in the lead, followed by one from the 315th and then two each from the 314th, 313th and 61st, and one from the 442nd TCG.

The Germans, now alerted, opened fire with everything they had, including small arms, at the C-47s at low altitude and slow speed as they emerged, silhouetted, against the moonlit overcast. C-47s started to go down. The tight formations became dispersed – there was no way they could come down through the clouds without losing contact with the serial lead ships (often the only ones with navigators), orient themselves and find the unmarked DZs, all the while losing speed and altitude. Many overshot the DZs, circling back to make another pass. One 314th TCG C-47's jumpmaster insisted on a third pass – it was shot down. Only four or five serials were able to keep formation. The paratroopers jumped from 500 ft, with the C-47s throttled back to 110 mph. A few jumped from 2000 ft, above the cloud deck.

One of the aircraft sortied on Mission 'Albany' by the 93rd TCS/439th TCG on 5-6 June 1944 was C-47 42-100876, piloted by 2Lt

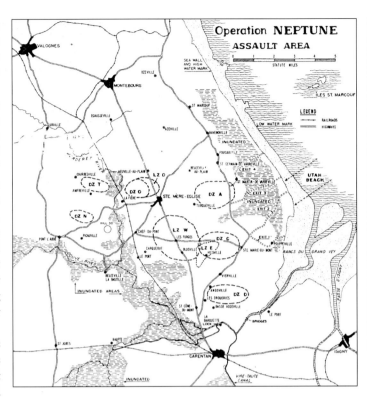

This map details the five drop zones and single glider landing zone for Operation *Neptune* (*Author's Collection*)

The goal of the mission – a stick of paratroopers drops away from a C-47 towards Normandy, as sketched by Capt Creekmore (*National Archives*)

Marvin F Muir. The remaining crewmembers were 2Lt Kenneth C Ball (co-pilot), SSgt Clifford Burgess (crew chief) and Sgt Philip Snyder (radio operator). Following the mission, the squadron intelligence officer wrote;

'While approaching the DZ in Normandy at about 0114 hrs on 6 June 1944, Lt Muir's aeroplane was hit by anti-aircraft fire near the companionway, and the baggage compartment (aft of the flight deck) was almost immediately filled with flames. The aeroplane wavered and then started to pull up straight as if the pilot was trying to get above the formation and give his paratroopers, and crew if possible, an opportunity to jump. Then it looked as though it stalled and fell first on the left wing and then on the right. A few seconds after the original fire, the left engine burst into flames. The aeroplane fell away to the right and went into a dive of about 30 degrees with level wings. Immediately, a stick of paratroopers were seen to emerge from the aeroplane. The speed of the aeroplane was in excess of normal landing speed – about 150 mph. It hit the ground at that angle in a burst of flame in the vicinity of the railroad a few miles southeast of Ste Mere Eglise, near the base of the Cherbourg Peninsula.'

There were no survivors from the crew – 17 of 18 paratroopers on board survived. For keeping the C-47 in the air long enough for the paratroopers to hook up and jump at the cost of his own life, 2Lt Muir was awarded a posthumous Distinguished Service Cross.

The crew of C-47 42-100849 of the 94th TCS/439th TCW pose for the camera just before taking off from Upottery on 5 June 1944. The '76' scrawled onto the side of the C-47 designates which 'chalk' of troops (in this case from the 506th PIR) would board the aircraft. They are 1Lt Harold King (pilot, centre), 1Lt Frank De Felitta (co-pilot, second left), 2Lt Thomas Waldman (navigator, right), TSgt Victor Zielinksi (crew chief, left, pointing) and Sgt Jerome Sterling (radio, second right). Note that De Felitta is wearing an armoured flak suit. More commonplace were standard GI helmets. The crew survived their D-Day mission and 42-100849 survived the war in the ETO, only to be condemned to salvage on 31 May 1946 (*Author's Collection*)

POOR DROP ACCURACY

Both missions ended up with the paratroopers scattered and dispersed. It was estimated several months later that of over 13,000 paratroops dropped, only some ten per cent landed on their DZ – the marked DZ 'Oboe' having the best accuracy. A further 25-30 per cent landed within a mile of their DZ and 15-20 per cent one to two miles away. A deviation of 2.5 degrees or minutes in navigation – the achievable level of accuracy – would put paratroopers five miles away from the DZ. The dense Norman countryside, divided by marshes and hedgerows, prevented the scattered US paratroopers from forming up quickly. While able to carry out most of their missions, losses were heavier than had been anticipated.

Before dawn, the paratroopers were followed by C-47 serials flying two night glider missions following the same routes. The 52 434th TCG C-47s, and their gliders, of Mission 'Chicago', carrying 101st troops, encountered mainly clear air. It followed Mission 'Albany's' route. Unexpected obstacles on LZ 'Easy' led to heavy casualties – only six of 39 gliders, mainly carrying airborne artillery, landed successfully on the LZ. The dead included the assistant divisional commander of the 101st Airborne. The 52 437th TCG C-47 glider tugs of Mission 'Detroit', carrying 82nd Airborne artillery to LZ 'Oboe', dispersed trying to fly through the cloud bank and were widely scattered. Some gliders released in the cloud bank, landing far to the west. Only half got into action – 17 gliders made it to LZ 'Oboe'.

The return flight – avoiding the invasion fleet – brought the C-47s off the east coast of Normandy at point 'Paducah', turning north to point 'Spokane', before following the beacon back to 'Gallup' and reversing the course back to their bases. Before D-Day dawned – the last paratroopers dropped at 0400 hrs – 925 C-47s had been committed to battle. Of the 821 dropping paratroops, 805 reached the DZ and 21 were lost. Of the 104 towing gliders, 103 reached their release points and two were lost.

CO's EXPERIENCES

Lt Col Charles H Young was commanding officer of the 439th TCG, and pilot of C-47A 43-15159 *The Argonia*, lead ship of the group on Mission 'Albany'. His crew consisted of 1Lt Adam Parsons (co-pilot), 2Lt Vincent Paterno (navigator), 2Lt Paul J Foynes (radar navigator), SSgt John A Doughty (radio operator) and SSgt Charles E Patterson (engineer), while the paratroopers on board included Col Robert Sink, commanding officer of the 506th PIR. Young's report of the mission read as follows;

'Take-off time 2315 hrs. Formation vee of vees in trail (439th formation divided into), Groups "A" and "B". Altitude en route 1500 ft-500 ft. Crossing the coast, outward bound, encountered scattered ships within ten-mile area of English coast. Several unidentified ships on course between the two marker boats, including one ship, probably a cruiser, one mile west of course just after passing first boat on route out. After leaving "Elko", we swung wide, and because of tail winds, had gained 1½ minutes by the time we had reached "Flatbush". Approaching Channel Islands, encountered flak from Alderney, large amount of flak from Guernsey. Saw small group of scattered ships about five miles east of Guernsey, heading 340 degrees, not known whether friendly or enemy.

'Just before we got to "Reno" (off the east coast of the Contentin peninsula), on the route out, there was a tremendous explosion in the centre of the peninsula and about four to five miles south of our course. After we left "Reno", on approaching the west coast of the peninsula, there was a layer of cloud that made us think it was land. We ran into this cloudbank three miles from the coast, but it was not apparent until it was too late to avoid it. I had to make a quick decision as to whether to try to climb up over this cloudbank or go beneath it, and I decided to climb up over it. I opened up to 40 inches (mercury of engine boost) to keep clear.

'No ground fire where we crossed beach. Encountered scattered fire, evidently rifle fire, from north and south along coast as I made landfall. None evidently from directly underneath, but heavy concentration of flak about eight miles inland

'About 11 miles inland, I found a hole through the clouds and went down on instruments again. I broke out through the cloud just past the first railroad, about one mile north. I passed just north of the intersection of the railroads and turned southeast as I saw the DZ, recognising it by the geographical features. There was no T (of ground lights) on the DZ, but there was Rebecca and also Gee. I saw the railroad, and the lake, as they appeared on the photo mosaic (map used for briefing).

'One mile right of course in vicinity of the lake and railroad – at about the four-minute red warning light (roughly eight miles west of DZ), there was a heavy concentration of flak from "four o'clock", with a mass of tracers, and at the same time there was a great deal of heavy flak bursting about ten miles to the north. Around the lake, to the right of the course, there was machine gun fire and tracers. Time over DZ 0108 hrs, at 700 ft altitude, 115-120 mph IAS (indicated air speed).

'About 30 seconds after I dropped at the DZ, we were in swamp land, and then I could see the causeways leading from the east beach back to the road which parallels Utah beach. There was no fire where we crossed the beach, but there was a good deal to the south of it.

'We dropped down to about 100 ft over the water, but that seemed a little low, so I climbed back up again to about 200 ft. There did not appear to be any life on St Marcouf Islands. After crossing St Marcouf Islands, there was flak along the northeast beach of the peninsula. Two minutes after crossing St Marcouf Islands, I saw a stream of tracers coming from "six o'clock", apparently from an aeroplane in the air. I would judge it was on the same level, or maybe a little higher, than we were, and our altitude was 400 ft. There was flak to the north of us along Utah beach, and we saw a stream of it after we left the beach. There was fire coming from all along the northeast tip of the peninsula, but apparently not aimed at us. When we were off Cherbourg, we also saw heavy flak.

'Saw three or four small ships after leaving "Paducah" on route back – three seemed to be anchored. We were at about 200 ft when we reached "Spokane" (off northeast corner of Contentin peninsula). At this point some of our own formation came up along with us. About 30 miles past "Spokane" the Gee equipment was jammed but still readable. As we approached "Gallup", several C-47s tacked on to our formation. As we approached the English coast, and when about ten miles out, we could see the light at Portland Bill. When we were at Portland we could see "Occult 31" (air navigation beacon). Landing 0237 hrs.

'The boys did an excellent job of formation flying. My wingmen stayed with me even when we moved up through and above the cloud. There were no lights on any DZ that I saw. My course over the DZ was about five degrees off the prescribed course, my heading being about 83 degrees magnetic. When we made landfall at the west side of the peninsula, we were about on course. I could see the reefs and could see the coast fairly clearly. As we got inland, I could not see the large forest, which was to the right of our course. I saw no barrage balloons at all. All my paratroopers jumped at the DZ, including Col Sink, and I had one door load which was thrown out. Just before I jumped the troopers, there was one searchlight off to the left of our course. The flak was heaviest in the vicinity of the lake, which was not far from the DZ.

'I request that in the future a weather ship should be sent out over the route that we are to fly a short time before our take-off so that we could get accurate weather information just before we leave. It might be arranged that the pathfinder aeroplanes could get this information back to us. In this particular case, if we had known the weather conditions on the course from the IP to the DZ, we could have flown at a lower altitude, and thus avoided some of the breaking up of the formation which occurred, and which resulted in the failure of some aeroplanes to drop accurately on the DZ.'

NORMANDY MISSIONS

Two twilight glider missions, intended to bring the rest of the airborne's divisional artillery, and heavily escorted by fighters, followed at around 2100-2250 hrs on D-Day. They were able to fly shorter, more direct routes from 'Gallup' to the LZs. Mission 'Keokuk', for the 101st, was flown by the 434th TCG C-47s towing 32 Horsas. Five landed right on the LZ, and most within two-and-a-half miles. Mission 'Elmira' was larger, with a first wave of two serials – 26 437th TCG C-47s towing eight CG-4As and 18 Horsas, and 50 438th TCG C-47s towing 14 CG-4As and 36 Horsas, to the 82nd at LZ 'William', which was under enemy fire.

The 82nd Airborne indicated by panels and markers that the gliders should be diverted to LZ 'Oboe'. Radio messages sent by the 82nd Airborne to divert the drop were not received by IX TCC, so the first wave landed scattered around LZ 'William' – only half of the CG-4As and a fifth of the Horsas remained intact. The second and third serials – 50 436th TCG C-47s towing two CG-4As and 48 Horsas and 48 435th TCG C-47s towing 12 CG-4As and 36 Horsas – continued on to LZ 'Oboe'. Both LZs remained under heavy fire in the failing daylight.

On the afternoon of 6 June 1944, a C-47 of the 90th TCS/438th TCG tows a Horsa aloft from Greenham Common's runway 11-29 as part of Mission 'Elmira' (*National Archives via Roger Freeman*)

7 June opened with the daylight glider reinforcement Missions 'Galveston' and 'Hackensack'. 'Galveston', for the 82nd, included 50 434th TCG C-47s towing 50 CG-4As, 50 437th TCG C-47s towing 32 CG-4As and 18 Horsas and two 435th TCG C-47s towing two Horsas. 'Hackensack', for the 101st, consisted of 50 439th TCG C-47s towing 20 CG-4As and 30 Horsas, and 50 441st TCG C-47s towing 50 CG-4As. 'Galveston' was diverted from LZ William to LZ Easy – jumping in daylight, landing casualties were minimised. 'Hackensack' pressed on to LZ William, despite heavy fire. They proved to be the most successful glider missions of the invasion, despite strong German opposition.

Two parachute resupply missions took place just after dawn on 7 June. Mission 'Freeport' saw 52 C-47s each from the 52nd TCW's four groups,

Several C-47s ditched while returning from the daylight missions flown on 7 June. Fortunately, the sea state had moderated from the day before. The crew of this C-47 were fortunate to have a rescue craft standing by while the aeroplane was still afloat. It was probably from the 440th TCG/95th TCG, hit by flak on Mission 'Memphis'. Its crew consisted of 1Lt John P Godwin (pilot), 2Lt Cyril Wire (co-pilot), 2Lt Richard P Umhoffer (navigator), SSgt Harold Blair (crew chief), SSgt Paul Shrull (radio) and T4 Irving MacDonald (war correspondent). The latter three were all killed while dropping supplies over DZ 'Easy' when a flak shell burst in the open cargo door. The others were picked up by boat. Wire received a Bronze Star for heroism in the rescue. Some C-47 crews had to spend up to three hours in dinghies on 7 June (*Author's Collection*)

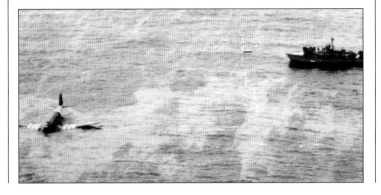

heading for DZ 'Nan' to resupply the 82nd Airborne. No fewer than 51 of the 208 C-47s sortied aborted en route due to bad weather, one crashing. Again, the 82nd tried to redirect the drop to DZ 'Oboe'. Some 148 C-47s dropped 156 of a planned 234 tons of supplies around DZs 'Oboe', 'Nan' and 'William', and two-thirds of the supplies were recovered and used by the 82nd. Eleven C-47s were lost. Mission 'Memphis' was the morn-

ing resupply mission to the 101st, which was not ready to receive it. The 148 C-47s from the 440th and 442nd TCGs encountered heavy German flak, which downed three C-47s and damaged 92 more. The 200 tons of supplies were widely scattered, with little recovered.

One of the participants in Mission 'Freeport' was 1Lt Vincent B 'Jack' Chiodo, a C-47 pilot with the 32nd TCS/314th TCG who was flying in the right seat of aircraft '396'. Alongside him was 1Lt Winford Taylor of the 314th TCG HQ. The remaining crewmen were Lt Isadore Caplan (navigator) and Sgt Harry D Ray (crew chief). Chiodo took off from Saltby early on 7 June and encountered bad weather that disrupted the formation. He recalled;

'Near Burbank, my ship lost the formation and we rejoined Maj Falkner at "Flatbush". Between "Gallup" and "Spokane" (Mission "Freeport" flew the direct rout), Lt Taylor took over the pilot's seat and I went into the co-pilot's seat. Our IP was approximately due east of DZ "Nan", and we crossed the coast at approximately 500 ft. Ship "146" was flying on Maj Falkner's right wing and my ship was on his left.

'My time over the DZ was approximately 0619 hrs. As we came over DZ "Nan", Maj Falkner dropped, and we dropped our bundles. Maj Falkner made a 180-degree turn and we followed. While we were in the turn, the whole wing tip on the right wing was bent down. Immediately thereafter, Lt Taylor stated that he had been hit. We were at 500 ft.

'I do not know whether the right wing was damaged in a mid-air collision (it was, with Maj Falkner's ship, hit by ground fire and going down), or whether it was due to enemy fire. At 200 ft I regained control of the ship and it was over the Douvre River. I had great difficulty in controlling the ship, and caught considerable machine gun fire along the Douvre River. At Ste Somme due Mont, I was beginning to get better control of the ship, and took a northeasterly course from there and came out over "Paducah". About three miles north of "Paducah" I

C-47s of the 88th TCS/438th TCG tow CG-4A gliders across Varreville, on the Normandy coast, to DZ 'William' as part of Mission 'Elmira', staged on 6 June. Just below the tail of the trailing C-47 is former German strongpoint W10, then occupied by the US 4th Infantry Division. The 88th TCS succeeded in getting all but one of its CG-4As onto the LZ in 'Elmira' (*National Archives via S Zaloga*)

This C-53 made it back to base with its outer right wing gone as a result of a 1942 mid-air collision (in the US), much like 'Jack' Chiodo's C-47 in Mission 'Freeport' (*National Archives*)

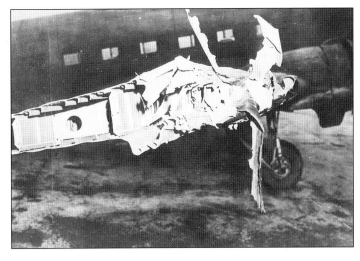

saw gliders coming in towards me. A P-47 picked me up in the vicinity of "Paducah" and stayed with me until I reached the English coast. The crew administered first aid to Lt Taylor.

'About five miles from "Paducah" my right engine cut out and picked up again when I switched tanks. I flew with 37 inch (mercury of boost pressure) on my right engine and 35 on my left, and was in a right skid all the way home.

'I managed to attain an altitude of 1200 ft by the time I had reached the English coast. Upon spotting

Warmwell, I was going to make a crash-landing, but decided against it and made a satisfactory wheel landing. I landed at Warmwell at 0720 hrs.'

This remains an immediate, but highly laconic and understated, description of a pilot – with the aid of his crew – having the skill to take full advantage of the C-47's structural strength. Falkner and his crew crash-landed and were made prisoners. Taylor survived. Chiodo was awarded the DFC.

On 6-7 June, 1683 C-47s (and 512 gliders) had been despatched for the invasion, 1,606 C-47s making it to their objectives (and 503 gliders to their release points). A total of 41 C-47s were lost or missing and 449 were damaged. The two-division US air assault of over 13,000 personnel had proven a success, despite the widespread scattering that increased casualties and undercut combat operations in the crucial opening days.

On 8-13 June C-47s flew several small-scale parachute and glider resupply missions to Normandy. A single 441st TCG C-47 dropped medicine on 8 June, and two gliders with replacement radios arrived for the 82nd Airborne the following day. The 436th TCG delivered six gliders on the 10th, and on 12 June nine more C-47s from the group dropped supplies and conducted five glider resupply mission. Another 11 gliders followed on 13 June.

The first mission into Normandy took place on 10 June. That same day, the first medical evacuation was flown by five 436th TCG C-47s from Laurent-sur-Mer, and regular sorties were started by the 31st TG the next day. Flight nurses and medical technicians from the Medical Air Evacuation Squadrons supplemented the C-47 crews, and within days transport and troop carrier groups were making regular resupply missions into forward airstrips, carrying priority cargo (mainly fuel and munitions for fighter-bombers) and leaving with casualties. But it was not until July, when a transport field was built at Querqueville and the medical evacuation system was better organised, that air evacuation by C-47s became widespread.

Participating in the first casualty evacuation mission from Normandy on 10 June 1944, C-47 42-24195 from the 82nd TCS/436th TCG was one of five flying to and from the forward strip at Laurent-sur-Mer, behind Omaha Beach, that day. The first day of casualty evacuations went badly – the C-47s were filled with anyone available, rather than a proper triage – but by July the system was more efficient (*National Archives*)

71st TCS C-47 42-24022 is loaded up at Greenham Common with blood supplies for delivery to Laurent-sur-Mer on 12 June 1944 (*National Archives via Roger Freeman*)

MTO 1944

In Italy, C-47 casualty evacuation missions – flying into forward airstrips and bringing back casualties to hospitals in Naples and Foggia – prevented lengthy overland medical evacuation. The 52nd TCW evacuated 202,000 personnel during its time in the MTO.

From Italian bases, C-47s also supported resistance movements in the Balkans, Greece and northern Italy. In February 1944, the 7th and 51st TCSs of the 62nd TCG moved to Brindisi, temporarily attached to the RAF's No 334 Wing. Three C-47s of the 51st TCS carried out Operation *Manhole* on 23 February, delivering three CG-4A gliders carrying a high-level Soviet and British liaison mission to the Yugoslav Partisans. Flown in daylight, with a large fighter escort, the gliders all landed successfully despite solid cloud over the LZ. Four days later, in Operation *Bunghole*, 7th TCS C-47s air-dropped US meteorologists to operate with the Partisans.

Starting in the spring, the 60th TCG's C-47s established a high mission tempo over the Balkans, averaging 35 sorties a night from April to October. Each C-47 airdropped (usually from 600 ft) about two tonnes of supplies, with the distribution of propaganda leaflets as a secondary mission. In addition to airdrops, increasingly frequent supply flights into liberated areas in Yugoslavia – starting in April 1944 – used unimproved airstrips. Wounded partisans and recovered Allied aircrew were flown out to Italy. The 60th alone flew 4,580 sorties to the Balkans, and lost ten C-47s. Other groups (plus the RAF and, later, an Italy-based Soviet C-47 squadron) contributed to the effort throughout 1944-45.

Two 51st TCW transports that were used in lifting Twelfth Air Force units to new bases in Corsica in 1944 formate for the camera. In the foreground is C-53 42-15880 *Woo's Woe*, and behind it is C-47 41-7847. *Woo's Woe*, a veteran of the North African campaign, stayed in Italy after the war. It was initially converted into an airliner, before reverting to its wartime role as a military transport. 41-7847 also enjoyed a long post-war career in Europe as a civil airliner, before being written off on 1 April 1981 in Laredo, Texas (*National Archives*)

Partisan groundcrews load up a USAAF C-47 in Italy with food for a resupply mission to Yugoslavia in the summer of 1944 (*National Archives*)

OPERATION
ANVIL-DRAGOON

For the invasion of southern France, 416 C-47s detached from the 50th and 53rd TCWs and the Pathfinder Group were fitted with ferry tanks and deployed to bases in Italy from England, via Gibraltar and Morocco. Together with the MTO-based 51st TCW – now rejoined by the 64th TCG – they came under control of the Provisional Troop Carrier Air Division (PTCAD) on 16 July, which was led by the IX TCC's Brig Gen Paul

Photographed at Berane, in Yugoslavia, in late August 1944, a multi-aircraft mission of C-47s prepare to be unloaded by Partisans. Berane was a major resupply field in early 1944, and duly became an objective of the German summer offensive. While enemy ground forces were unable to hold it, Luftwaffe aircraft continued to bomb Berane by day and night in an effort to interrupt C-47 operations (*Boris Ciglic*)

Williams. The PTCAD was subordinated directly to the USSTAF.

The MTO-based C-47 crews had recently been moving the Twelfth Air Force to Corsica. They had not trained for a daylight formation airdrop since 1943, although several had been planned, and cancelled.

MTO C-47s had a lower priority for Rebecca and radar. This required the C-47 units deploying from England to take over casualty evacuation and intratheatre transport missions in Italy while the 51st TCW trained and modified C-47s. Yet the England-based units had themselves carried out few training missions since D-Day. They had received additional radars – two per squadron – and Gee. The first US-built Loran sets (similar to Gee) had also been fitted. Glider towing training had been scarcer, most MTO glider pilots having been sent to England before D-Day. The high attrition of gliders on 6 June led to training missions being cut back to reduce losses. Pilots were instead flown to Italy from England for pre-invasion training.

After plans for a deep air assault to seize an airhead at Avignon and dispersed airdrops along the coast had been rejected, the *Anvil-Dragoon* plan centred on a concentrated assault on four DZ/LZs. The US-British 1st Airborne Task Force (the size of a small division) would drop at dawn, following pathfinders. The drop would be supported by a pre-assault deception mission by five RAF Dakotas dropping dummy paratroopers, electronic warfare support by jamming aircraft, fighter escorts and flak suppression missions. A scaled-down rehearsal was held on 7 August, aimed at exercising navigational aids and coordination with naval forces. Radio beacons were installed along the route, including three on ships.

On 15 August pathfinder C-47s left Italian bases at 0100 hrs. They found their DZs shrouded in fog, and only those intended for DZ 'Oboe' landed on their objective and marked it. Those bound for DZ 'Able' landed several miles away. Encountering opposition, they did not mark until the afternoon. DZ 'Charlie' pathfinders landed 15 miles distant.

Mission 'Albatross' included ten serials with some 296 USAAF and RAF transports carrying 5600 paratroopers, scheduled to arrive an hour after the pathfinders. The first serial – 45 C-47s from the 442nd TCG – headed for DZ 'Charlie', between Nice and Marseilles. While it was unmarked, good radar and visual navigation by the lead C-47s put most paratroopers within a half-mile of the DZ. The second serial of 45 C-47s from the 441st TCG dropped on unmarked DZ 'Able' and scattered paratroopers in the cloud. The third through seventh serials, intended to be concentrated on DZ 'Able', had to drop by dead reckoning and radar, scattering paratroopers. The tail-end of the mile-long formation, mainly from the 51st TCW, dropped the British at well-marked DZ 'Oboe'.

Mission 'Bluebird' – the glider lift – was already formed up and en route to the LZs when it received radio reports from the lead ships of 'Albatross' of unexpected ground fog that left only the tops of hills visible. 'Bluebird's' first serial of 35 435th TCG C-47s, towing Horsas, were ordered by Gen Williams to abort the mission. The second serial of 436th TCG C-47s, towing 33 CG-4As, were able to circle, waiting for the fog to burn off. The gliders made it to DZ 'Oboe' at about 0930 hrs. Later in the day the 35 Horsas held over from the morning were towed to LZ 'Oboe' without incident.

That same afternoon, Mission 'Canary' saw 41 437th TCG C-47s drop 736 paratroops over DZ 'Able', which was now marked. Mission 'Dove' followed, with seven serials of C-47s towing 332 CG-4As to LZs 'Able' and 'Oboe'. The planners did not allow the huge formation enough manoeuvring room, and there were problems with Rebecca-Eureka and premature glider releases. Despite good

conditions, the glider landings into over-crowded LZs were confused – glider losses were heavy, although personnel casualties were relatively light. In Mission 'Eagle', flown after dawn on 16 August, 112 53rd TCW C-47s dropped 246 tons of supplies over the now well-marked DZs 'Able' and 'Oboe' despite encountering problems with cargo handling equipment. Some 60 per cent of the drop proved to be recoverable. Later that day, 30 51st TCW C-47s made three separate on-call resupply drops. Only a single C-47 was lost to enemy action, ditching after 'Dove'.

An unidentified navigator of the 4th TCS/62nd TCG on 'Albatross' and 'Dove' made the following report for the unit's war diary;

'If it hadn't been for our radar and Eureka equipment this morning, that invasion would have been classified as a big flop. With the target completely covered by a heavy undercast, radar was the only means of finding the drop zone. It was the biggest responsibility I ever had.

'I can just imagine how those paratroopers riding in our aeroplane were sweating me out. I sure am glad to hear our drops were recorded as 100 per cent successful. It didn't take the Germans long to set up anti-aircraft batteries along our course, because when we made our second trip over France this afternoon, there they were, waiting for us. It took plenty of work to dodge their fire, but it was worth it with the record we made.'

The first medical evacuation C-47 landed in southern France on 22 August. The Allied advance up the Rhone Valley required extensive air resupply as it outran its supply lines, with these missions being carried out for weeks later after the IX TCC C-47s returned. The 51st TCW remained in the MTO to fly these missions, while the 50th and 53rd TCW C-47s started to fly back to England, via Gibraltar, from 20 August. The 51st TCW continued to fly resupply and casualty evacuation missions into southern France until 15 November.

A serial of multiple nine-ship vee-of-vees formations heads on its way to southern France during *Anvil-Dragoon*. The aircrafts' undersurface invasion stripes identify these as IX TCC C-47s (*National Archives*)

Mission 'Canary' saw 41 C-47s from the 437th TCG drop 736 paratroopers over DZ 'Able' after the morning fog that had blighted the early morning sorties had largely burned away (*National Archives*)

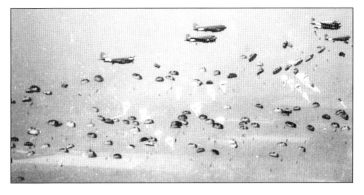

LIBERATION

Air resupply to ground forces became vital after the Normandy breakout, which commenced on 25 July. In the heavy fighting which followed, C-47s were used for parachute resupply to ground units. Airdrops to the units of the 30th Infantry Division enabled them to defend critical positions around Mortain against German counterattacks on 8-13 August.

The rapid liberation of France and Belgium following the defeat of organised German resistance in Normandy was made possible by air resupply – some air-dropped, but most flown into ex-Luftwaffe airfields. C-47s delivered an average of 2000 tons a day, primarily fuel. Most aircraft carried 120 five-gallon jerrycans of gasoline, all loaded and unloaded manually. 'Hap' Arnold ordered ten ATC C-47s to be pressed into service for this effort, pulled from scheduled flights. Additionally, in August, the ATC rushed 100 C-47s and 150 crews from the US as reinforcements for the ETO's Transport Groups. The C-47s were supplemented by B-24s of the Eighth Air Force's 2nd Air Division used as fuel tankers. In September, B-24s carried a quarter of the 40,000 tons airlifted to the ground forces.

Commitment of IX TCC to resupply tasks had limited its training with airborne forces. In the four days before the opening of Operation *Market-Garden* (13-16 September), IX TCC flew over 1900 transport sorties, delivering 5300 tons of supplies and evacuating 1891 casualties.

The rapid advance increased the importance of casualty evacuation. Since April 1944, all new-production C-47 had been delivered with web-strap litter supports, allowing the aircraft to be quickly changed to medical evacuation configuration. Such supports were also widely retrofitted. By September, ten specialist air medical evacuation units were in the ETO. While there were never enough C-47s to give them their own dedicated red-cross aeroplanes, their specialist personnel – especially flight nurses – were soon flying missions. Improved planning brought casualties to forward airfields at the same time as resupply C-47s were set to return to England.

An internal view of a C-47 loaded with five-gallon jerrycans bound for an airfield at Orleans, in France, in the late summer of 1944. Although not an efficient or safe way of lifting gasoline – filling and static discharge accidents claimed a number of C-47s – the fuel airlift was critical to the Allied advance across France in the summer of 1944 (*National Archives*)

A Transport Group C-47 taxies down the pierced steel planking runway at Querqueville, in Normandy, in July-August 1944 at the end yet another resupply flight from England (*National Archives*)

The ATC European Wing opened services to Paris soon after its liberation. The 27th and 31st TGs (with 184 aircraft) were linked on 1 September under the 302nd TW, subordinated to USSTAF. This arrangement was originated by Maj Gen Hugh Knerr, now Deputy Commander for Administration, USSTAF. He also put IX TCC under USSTAF control, thus centralising ETO C-47s. The Ninth Air Force replaced the 31st TG with the 1st TG (Provisional) on 1 September.

First Allied Airborne Army (FAAA) was formed on 8 August, directly under SHAEF (Supreme Headquarters Allied Expeditionary Forces) headquarters. It was intended to provide better integration of aircraft and ground forces. Lt Gen Lewis Brereton, formerly commander of the Ninth Air Force (who had been the staff officer in 1918 that planned 1919 parachute drops) took command. Within one week, FAAA had operational control of IX TCC, plus US and British airborne divisions. CATOR also initially came under FAAA control, although by October it was directly under SHAEF. The USAAF and RAF transport groups, as well as the ATC, stayed beyond FAAA's grasp. The CTCCP served to link them with IX TCC.

FAAA's focus on strategic air assaults led to tensions with the need to use IX TCC C-47s for resupply of ground and air forces, and casualty evacuation. In its first six weeks of existence, FAAA planned for, and cancelled, no less than 18 airborne operations. When the Troop Carrier Groups had to stand down, rig their C-47s for airdrops and do refresher training or rehearsals, it made them unavailable for resupply and casualty evacuation missions – the groups then had to carry that burden.

Higher headquarters moved from England to the Continent. A 75-sortie C-47 airlift moved SHAEF HQ to Paris in September. C-47 units were heavily committed in moving tactical air units to new bases on the continent which were remote from the logistics support network that had been built up for them in the UK, and therefore needed sustained airlift support. While bulk cargoes – aviation fuel and bombs – largely came via surface transport, competing with the Army's need for tonnage, C-47s provided other needs. But even with intense transport aircraft support, the operational availability rate of C-47s based on the continent was below that of those based in Britain. The same problem re-occurred in southern France when the 1st Allied Tactical Air Force arrived. It needed C-47s to link it to support and logistics facilities.

Well-worn 314th TCG C-47s enjoy a brief respite at Saltby between shuttle missions to the Normandy beachhead in August 1944. The two aircraft closest to the camera feature mission logs above the fuselage windows (*National Archives via Roger Freeman*)

Starting soon after D-Day, the USAAF also had to deal with damaged aircraft that managed to land on forward airfields. C-47s carried repair teams – organised at different levels from bases through sub-depots to base air depots – to fly new engines and parts to these aircraft. Originally at Transport Group mission, some were flown by borrowed Troop Carrier Group aircraft. Service units also reinforced their pre-existing flights of C-47s (often overhauled troop carrier veterans) with improvised crews.

C-47 SPECIAL OPERATIONS

From Leuchers, ATC C-47s, tiny US civil registrations stencilled on their olive drab paint, were among the Allied aircraft operating between Britain and neutral Sweden. In Operation *Sonnie*, ATC C-47s (reinforcing five converted B-24s) flew out interned Allied aircrew and Norwegian refugees over German-occupied Norway. The operation, in March-December 1944, succeeded with the loss of a single aircraft. In Operation *Big Ben*, an ATC C-47 was used to carry out a crashed prototype German V 2 ballistic missile that had come down in Sweden in June 1944 and was turned over to the Allies.

USAAF special operations based in England, codenamed *Carpetbagger*, used a limited number of Eighth Air Force C-47s. Part of the 801st (redesignated 492nd) BG, most C-47 missions were flown within Britain, collecting agents and cargoes to be dropped over occupied Europe by the group's modified B-24s. Starting on 8 July, four radar-equipped C-47s were also used to fly directly to improvised landing strips in Europe. Before the start of Operation *Market* (17 September), they had flown 35 sorties, delivering 62 tons of munitions and evacuating 213 passengers. After *Market*, these C-47s were operationally tasked by the Office of Strategic Services (OSS), transferring personnel and supplies to and from the continent.

The attempt to set up the Eastern Air Command of the USSTAF in Soviet territory for shuttle bombing from British and Italian bases, codenamed Operation *Frantic*, was enabled by ATC and USSTAF C-47 operations. Between the (reluctant) Soviet agreement in February 1944 and the first US bombers landing in Ukraine in June, the ATC had lifted in 450 personnel and 18 tons of cargo, including critical radio navigation beacons. Limited by the Soviets to two round-trips weekly, ATC, MATS and Transport Group C-47s supported shuttle bombing missions for the rest of the war.

In late 1944, German forces were withdrawing from northern Norway and Finland under pressure from the advancing Soviets. Sweden gave permission for a para-military Norwegian police battalion that had been organised there during the war to be airlifted into northern Norway and resupplied by USAAF C-47s. These aircraft were also used for

'We have aeroplanes just like that, but with different engines'. A group of Soviet Air Force officers admire the engines – which distinguished it from their license-built Li-2 version – of a C-47 at Poltava on 2 May 1945. The yellow and black checked cowling identifies the Rebecca-equipped aircraft as belonging to the 320th TS/27th TG. A 31st TG C-47 is parked in the background (*National Archives*)

Operations *Sepal* and *Where-and-Why*, lifting supplies for the Norwegian resistance to Swedish bases, and for supply drops inside Norway.

Operation *Ball* started with nine C-47As and one C-47B of the 27th TG arriving in Sweden on 29 December, commanded by USAAF Col Bernt Balchen, the pre-war polar aviator who had previously supervised Operation *Sonnie*. The C-47s moved to Kallaz airfield, where the Norwegian battalion was based, and in January 1945 started airlifting them to Kierkenes, then occupied by the Soviets. Despite diplomatic friction, and attempts by enemy fighters to intercept the C-47s, the airlift was successful, and was followed by the airlift of a hospital and resupply missions. C-47s carried 1500 personnel and 360 tons of supplies from Sweden into northern Norway until the mission ended in August 1945.

OPERATION *MARKET-GARDEN*

Operation *Market-Garden* was a massive airborne drop (*Market*) linking up with a ground advance (*Garden*) by British XXX Corps through the Netherlands and across the Rhine. C-47s were key to the planned three-day operation. The FAAA staff was confident that IX TCC, and their RAF, counterparts could insert and sustain an airborne force deep in the enemy's rear area. The RAF – with USAAF support – would have the primary responsibility for the British 1st Airborne Division, which was to land near the Rhine crossings at Arnhem. IX TCC would insert and sustain the 101st Airborne at Eindhoven and the 82nd Airborne at Nijmegen. Reinforcements were ready to be airdropped (Polish 1st Airborne Brigade) or air landed (British 52nd Infantry Division) by IX TCC.

Planning reflected Normandy and southern France lessons, with the initial landings being in daylight. Routes from bases in England were divided into parallel lanes for two-way air traffic, with different altitudes and routes being reserved for gliders, marked with beacons and navigation aids.

The hastily planned operation – there had been no dress rehearsal and limited group-level training due to heavy commitments to the transport mission – opened on 17 September. Four pairs of pathfinder C-47s were the first to take-off. They succeeded in dropping their paratroopers, who marked the DZs. A total of 1546 transports (mainly C-47s) and 478 gliders took off from 24 airfields in England in the initial lift. C-47s flew in standard nine-ship vee-of-vees formation. Serials of up to 45 aircraft flew in

This map details the main battle area for the ambitious Operation *Market-Garden* (*Author's Collection*)

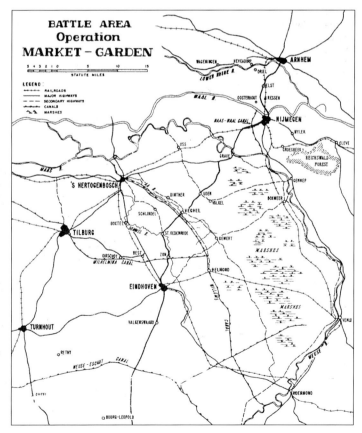

trail with four minutes separation. Glider tugs flew in pairs of pairs, with just seven-minute intervals between the serials, up to 48 strong. The two columns, routed to avoid flak concentrations, were divided into three streams, offset to provide a mile-and-a-half separation.

On the southern route, the 53rd TCW sent 11 serials with 424 C-47s carrying paratroopers and towing 70 glider tugs for the 101st. On the northern route, the 50th and 52nd TCWs dropped the 82nd from 11 serials with 480 C-47s, plus 50 towing gliders. The 61st and 314th TCGs' 147 C-47s reinforced the RAF at Arnhem. The initial drops went well.

Fighters provided escort and bombers carried out flak suppression. Losses – 35 transports and 13 gliders – were mainly from serials heading for DZ/LZs near Eindhoven, closest to the forward edge of the battle area. A total of 5000 troop carrier and 2400 glider missions were flown on the first day alone.

Participating in *Market-Garden* was 1Lt John R Gurecki Jr, who was the pilot of 80th TCS/436th TCG C-47A 42-24066;

'Five minutes out of the designated DZ things started to happen. The navigator had just finished saying "here it comes" when our aeroplane started swaying as a result of bursting flak. Black puffs could be seen quite frequently beneath and a little ahead of us, evidencing a thick layer of flak which we knew we had to override. The aeroplane vibrated several times and we knew that we had been hit by both flak and small arms fire. We flew on for about three minutes, which seemed like hours. Optimism began then to overtake us, for we felt that the worst must surely be over.

'It was then that the navigator and co-pilot chimed out almost simultaneously that the aeroplane was afire. At the same time smoke

Paratroopers from the 82nd Airborne Division prepare to board a 44th TCS/316th TCG C-47 at Cottesmore on the eve of Operation *Market-Garden* in September 1944 (*National Archive via Roger Freeman*)

Waiting for *Market-Garden* to commence, C-47s of the 45th TCS/316th TCG sit nose to tail on one of the Cottesmore taxiways on 16 September 1944 (*National Archives*)

A 'cab rank' of 89th TCS C-47s await their human cargo at Greenham Common on the eve of *Market-Garden*. Heading the line is 42-100766, which was condemned to salvage on 25 October 1944 (*National Archive via Roger Freeman*)

The 36th TCS/316th TCG heads on its way to Nijmegen on 17 September 1944. The lead ship (third from left) has an SCR-717C radome under its belly. 43-15179 *Buddy* (closest to the camera) and the rest of the formation were part of Serial A-9, carrying the 1-504th PIR to DZ 'Oboe'. *Buddy* survived *Market-Garden*, but went down in flames on 3 April 1945, hit by flak on a fuel resupply mission. Its pilot, Col Harvey A Berger, commanding officer of the 316th TCG, stayed at the controls. He was overcome by smoke and died after rescuing the co-pilot following a crash landing. All the remaining crewmembers survived (*Author's Collection*)

began coming through the floor fairly thick. In spite of the fire, and the unceasing gunfire from below, I maintained my formation position in an effort to get the aeroplane, and especially the personnel, over the flak area. Just before we got to the intended position we were hit again, this time in the right engine, rendering our aeroplane just about useless. The gas line must have been hit too, for it would no longer take when the throttles were applied.

'A lot happened in these two minutes, but now we were finally over the flak area. I found that I could no longer keep with the speed of the other ships in the formation, so I proceeded to nose the aeroplane down to a level a few feet below 436th TCG CO Col Adriel Williams' ship in order that the personnel would not be overrun by the aeroplanes to our rear as they jumped out. It was now that I gave the green light for the paratroops to jump, and I ordered the crew to jump as well.

'While they were jumping, I cut the mixture controls back and switched off both engines to prevent a possible explosion. This naturally put the aeroplane in a pretty fast glide, but I held it up as best I could until all of them finally got out. All of this was accomplished at an altitude of 300 ft. I looked back into the fuselage to make doubly certain that there wasn't anyone remaining, and all I could see was a lot of smoke and flames starting to inch their way through the compartment where the navigator sat. With this sight in the back of my mind, it is hard to explain the feeling of satisfaction that suddenly came over me just to know that I was responsible for only one person – myself.

'At approximately 150 ft, I reached over and put the flaps down to the full flap position. All that remained now was the actual landing, which I was rapidly approaching. I found myself heading for several cows, so I immediately kicked the rudder in order to change my direction. In the next change of direction, I found myself heading for a house, so I had to kick the rudder again, while all the time looking for a large enough

clearing to set it down, but to no avail.

'By this time there wasn't much left to do but actually land, so I picked the largest opening I could find and not long after I hit. I struck my eye, and it seemed to me that that was all there was to it, but actually I slid about three aeroplane lengths, which even now I cannot account for because it happened so quickly. My eye was bleeding freely, and I realised that the next thing to do was to make an exit, but fast. I turned around and saw the whole companionway was enveloped in flames, so I freed myself of all of my equipment, covered my face to prevent it from being burned and ran through to the back of the aeroplane, and into good old terra firma.

'About three yards from the aeroplane was a ditch, about four feet deep, into which I immediately jumped for cover. I ran for about 20 yards in a crouched position over a barbed wire fence into another field. When I felt that I was far enough from the aeroplane, I looked up, only to stare into the face of another pilot who had also been forced down intact. We ran for cover. We took the nearest thing gladly, for not many seconds later, and continuing for two solid hours, was continuous mortar fire over the top of us in an effort to knock out some German tanks and vehicles. By this time the paratroops advanced close to us, so we linked up with them and soon after were on our way to a field hospital. It rained that night, so we were crammed into a tent, where we spent the night.'

1Lt Gurecki's landing was so spectacular that it was reported as non-survivable, and several historical accounts still list him as killed in action!

The continued shortage of USAAF C-47 aircrew, and the decision not to mount night operations, limited the England-based crews to one sortie a day after the initial assault, even though the airborne commanders had argued for two. As the battle dragged on, crew fatigue became a factor, even at one lift per day.

The weather closed in on 18 September, blocking the southern fly-in route and delaying the planned reinforcement and resupply mission until the afternoon. Last-minute replanning was required to launch 1336 C-47 resupply sorties (plus 340 RAF), 1305 of them towing gliders, joined by 252 B-24s dropping supplies. The 314th and 315th TCGs sent 114 C-47s to Arnhem.

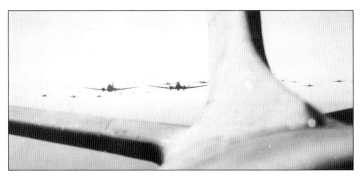

A trailing formation of 349th TCG C-47s flies the return leg of the initial lift of *Market-Garden* on 17 September 1944. The good weather evident here was not to last (*National Archives*)

Ready to transport 388 paratroops of the 82nd Airborne Division to Holland, C-47s from the 439th TCG are lined up at Balderton on 17 September 1944. Note the SCR-717 ground-mapping radar radome beneath the fuselage of the C-47 (43-15159) closest to the camera. This aircraft was flown by the group CO, Lt Col Charles H Young (*via Roger Freeman*)

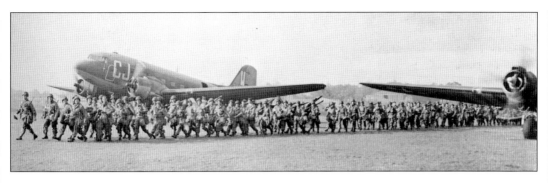

Men of the 101st Airborne Division are led out to their aircraft at Aldermaston on 17 September 1944. Already idling, the C-47s that flank the paratroops are from the 71st TCS/434th TCG. The aircraft were bound for the drop zones near Veghel (*National Archive via Roger Freeman*)

The main glider missions – the 53rd TCW towing 450 for the 101st and the 52nd TCW (plus the 439th TCG) towing 454 for the 82nd – went relatively well, although the later serials suffered from scattering. Up to 80 per cent of the supplies dropped by the 50th and 52nd TCWs to the 82nd Airborne near Nijmegen were recovered, despite problems with Gee (jamming) and Rebecca/Eureka (interference).

Other drops (including the B-24s) proved less effective, reflecting the breakdown of communications between the paratroopers and Britain, especially at Arnhem, where the 52nd TCW was again committed to the second lift into LZs that proved too distant from the ground objectives. Of the 1306 transports and 1152 gliders despatched on 18 September, 22 transports and 21 gliders were lost.

Bad weather on 19 September limited C-47 operations, with the 52nd TCW's mission to airdrop the Polish 1st Airborne Brigade near Arnhem being among the many scrubbed that day. The 53rd TCW (and 442nd TCG) postponed its glider mission until the afternoon, launching 353 C-47s towing gliders for the 101st. As weather deteriorated, many C-47s aborted and gliders broke free. Only 213 made it to the DZ, although most landed safely. Flak claimed 17 C-47s on this mission alone.

Capt Edward J Vosika of the 81st TCS/436th TCG was a combat veteran and pilot of a C-47 on the glider mission to Eindhoven on 19 September. His crew was made up of 2Lt Martin Jacobson (co-pilot), 2Lt Howard Johnson (navigator), SSgt Willis Shumake (crew chief) and TSgt Warren Runyan (radio operator). Vosika recalled;

'On the glider mission of 19 September take-off was at 1201 hrs. Visibility and ceiling were low. Because of this, we had great difficulty keeping in formation.

'When crossing the Channel, the weather became much worse, and we had to fly at 100 ft so that the glider could see us. We lost our leader,

The last moments of a C-47, dramatically captured on film near Zon. The date of this photograph is uncertain, but it probably shows 1Lt Jesse Harrison's aeroplane of the 435th TCG going down on 19 September. His C-47 was hit on the way to the LZ, but still towed its glider to the briefed cut-off point. Only then did the crew bail out. The crew chief jumped too late and was killed. Harrison had previously been awarded the DFC for heroism on D-Day (*National Archives*)

A C-47 goes down near Nijmegen, its lack of self-sealing tanks being clearly evident. IX TCC's heroic efforts during *Market-Garden* accounted for a substantial percentage of the total USAAF C-47 losses in the ETO (*National Archives*)

The enemy in *Market-Garden* – a German war artists' impression of a 37 mm SP flak gun in action against a low-angle target. To survive in the face of Allied air superiority, the Germans deployed massive numbers of flak guns, both in Germany and with their forces in the field. The decision – after the D-Day scattering – to rely on day airdrops in *Market-Garden* forced the C-47s to run the gauntlet of such weapons. While Ninth Air Force fighter-bombers provided flak suppression strikes, these were limited by concerns over Dutch civilian casualties (*National Archives*)

Lt Col David Brack (the squadron CO), but after crossing the coast of France the weather improved a little and we found him – he was leading our wave. We were very nearly on course on the route, but when we turned to run-in, we seemed to be left of course.

'About halfway between the IP and LZ, we were hit by a barrage of fire – probably 20 mm, judging from the size of the holes in the wings. The right engine was knocked out, and we had holes in both wings and right aileron, and also in the empennage. Some hits were also received in the fuselage. Col Brack was hit just before this and lost his glider.

'At this time I looked back from my seat and saw smoke coming from the floor. At this time I gave the bail out order, as I didn't know how long it would be before the aeroplane would explode. And from the smoke, I knew we were afire.

'We flew on a heading of 220 degrees for approximately five minutes, and saw another formation approaching on course for the LZ, so I called Lt Byrum and Lt Braden, who now had taken position on my wing, and I told them to follow me into the LZ. They replied "Okay". While turning, we climbed to about 2500 ft. Now we started turning to come into position on the tail of the other formation, descending at the same time.

'No sooner had we turned to a course of 44 degrees than Lt Byrum called and said I was on fire. The right engine had started to flame. So we bailed out at about 2000 ft over the Albert Canal and landed on the west side of the canal in Allied territory. The three crew members who bailed out first had evidently jumped about 10 to 15 miles northeast of the Albert Canal, judging from my position, and the time we flew on a course of 220 degrees – they were captured.

'In about 15 minutes I had contacted Lt Jacobson, who bailed out with me, and a British sergeant found us. He took us to our crashed C-47, where we made sure no papers or secret or confidential equipment was left, and then he took us to a battalion HQ. They provided us with transportation to a brigade HQ, where we were fed and quartered. There we found out that our glider pilot had cut off when he saw the flames and had landed okay. He cut loose at about 2500 ft. The glider personnel had gone to the front to join their unit.

'The next morning (20 September) we were taken to Brussels airport, (B 56), where we contacted the US communications officer and he sent in a TWX of our reporting. We were unable to get a ride to the UK that day, so we were provided food and lodging in a hotel rest camp in Brussels. The following morning we returned to the field and got a ride on a British aircraft to Down Ampney. There, we contacted Sqn Ldr Brodie, who contacted Col Tobiason and an aeroplane was sent for us. We returned to this station on 21 September at about 1600 hrs.'

Only 60 C-47 parachute resupply sorties were flown on 19 September, mainly to the 82nd. Gee jamming

Personnel of the ten ETO medical air evacuation and treatment squadrons were the 'rear end' crew on Troop Carrier and Transport Group C-47 casualty evacuation missions, often assisted by aircrew. Standing in this shot are (from left to right) USAAF flight nurses 2Lts Anna Ranshan, Ethyl Guffey, Marion Hammesch, Dorothy Barlow, Florence Deluca and Mary McHugh. Kneeling are enlisted medical technicians SSgt Emory Craver, Sgt Kenneth Schulze and Harold Stockseth (*National Archives*)

made navigation difficult (especially for the RAF, who relied on it). Rebecca/Eureka worked better. Weather and reinforced flak reduced the air dropped supplies recovered to 20 per cent. The need to manhandle supplies out the doors of C-47s often made multiple passes over the DZs necessary. A further three C-47s went down on this mission.

Operations on the 20th were curtailed due to weather. Nevertheless, some 357 C-47s were dispatched to resupply the US airborne, including 310 53rd TCW C-47s sent to the 82nd to airdrop ammunition. The bad visibility led to scattered drops, however, and at Arnhem German advances kept RAF-dropped supplies from reaching the troops.

On 21 September the weather was still bad, but 114 C-47s of the 314th and 315th TCGs were finally able to drop the Poles at a new DZ near Driel. A mistaken recall signal split one serial, and there was difficulty in locating the DZ. Heavy flak disrupted the formation, returning at low altitude. The drop was 50 per cent effective. Five C-47s were shot down.

Other missions were cancelled because of the weather, and many of the aircraft that were launched could not find the DZs – of 174 C-47 sorties, 49 had to abort. But the 53rd TCW was able to drop rations from 24 C-47s to the 101st and 31 to the 82nd.

The weather continued to deteriorate, and on 22 September all C-47 missions were cancelled. A brief break in the weather the following day saw the despatch of 406 C-47-towed 50th and 52nd TCW gliders for the 82nd that had been held ready for four days, plus 84 from the 53rd TCW for the 101st. The remainder of the Polish brigade was dropped by the 315th TCG near Nijmegen, while the RAF kept up Arnhem missions. Fighter escorts beat back Luftwaffe attempts at interception, but nine C-47s were lost to flak. The gliders arrived in good condition, except for a formation of six that had released prematurely and ended up in a German strongpoint. The weather then closed in again, preventing any C-47 missions on 24 September, and cancelling all but one parachute resupply mission to the 101st by 34 53rd TCW C-47s on 25 September.

The remnants of 1st Airborne were ordered to withdraw back across the Rhine on 23 September – this was carried out 48 hours later. Immediately after the withdrawal from Arnhem, it was planned to lift the British 52nd Division into the grass airstrip at Grave (near Nijmegen), now behind Allied lines, following a planned glider insertion of engineers, air control teams, and air defence artillery to improve and hold the airfield. This was converted, due to weather, into an airlanding mission – 209 C-47s delivered troops and supplies into the airstrip during the afternoon of 26 September, with up to 70 being unloaded around the tiny airfield at any one time. However, the fly-in of the 52nd Division was cancelled, and subsequent C-47 operations at Grave were

limited to a few resupply missions. It was the only occasion in the ETO that the concept of using C-47s to drop airborne forces to seize an airhead and then fly-in reinforcements came close to implementation.

By 26 September, 4242 USAAF transport and 1899 glider sorties had been flown, resulting in the loss of 98 C-47s (11 of them over Arnhem) and 137 gliders. IX TCC C-47s had suffered a loss rate of about 2.5 per cent. Large-scale fighter escort and flak suppression efforts – over 5200 sorties – made possible the daylight operations, with a further 87 bombers and fighters lost. Two Ninth Air Force P-47 groups suffered especially heavy losses flying flak suppression missions.

Following *Market-Garden*, the air resupply and casualty evacuation missions continued. Troop carrier and transport group C-47s evacuated over 26,000 patients in September alone. In October, 150 IX TCC C-47s were designated by USSTAF as primarily casualty evacuation aircraft when not required for FAAA missions. Transport Group C-47s later performed most of the medical evacuation missions, with four of the air medical squadrons transferring to ATC control. C-47s from the latter command also flew an increasing number of intratheatre casualty evacuation sorties, connecting with its transatlantic C-54 flights.

Each rigged up to carry two Waco assault gliders apiece, C-47s from the 80th TCS sit lined up on the main runway at Membury on 14 November 1944. Ultimately, the operation to which these aircraft were assigned was cancelled (*National Archives via Roger Freeman*)

A 434th TCG C-47 drops supplies to paratroops cut off during the defence of Bastogne in December 1944 (*National Archives*)

OPERATION *REPULSE*

Bad weather was critical to the initial German success in the Battle of the Bulge, starting on 16 December 1944. C-47s of IX TCC were loaded to drop supplies to cut-off US 106th Infantry Division troops, but the weather remained bad and the mission planning was unable to keep up with the battlefield situation. When the 106th was forced to surrender

on 22 December, the loaded C-47s were still sitting on French airfields.

The focus of the southern front of the battle had become the Belgian town of Bastogne, held by a strong, but isolated, US force built around the 101st Airborne Division. The aerial resupply of Bastogne, Code-named Operation *Repulse*, began on 23 December. Pathfinders were dropped from two C-47s to mark DZ/LZs and 260 C-47s made three drops in daylight – 50th TCW and Pathfinder Group drops in the morning and a major 53rd TCW drop in the afternoon. Because of the resurgence in German air activity, three Ninth Air Force fighter groups provided escorts to the afternoon mission. Eight C-47s were lost to flak.

C-47 42-100862 *Ain't Misbehavin'* of the 94th TCS/439th TCG bellied in on 27 December at Savy, near Bastogne, after being hit by flak during Operation *Repulse*

On the 24th, six C-47s inserted more pathfinders, followed by 160 C-47s from the 53rd TCW. They were able to airdrop accurately and without loss. Bad weather on 25 December prevented operations. The following day, despite bad weather, both the 50th and 53rd TCWs took part in three glider missions and a large daylight supply drops by 289 escorted C-47s (including 46 towing gliders). The first glider mission by the 440th TCG carried a medical unit to replace the 101st's field hospital, which had been overrun by the Germans.

On 27 December, 138 53rd TCW C-47s dropped supplies and towed 50 CG-4As, many carrying gasoline. Following the same route as the previous day, despite the Army having radioed in last minute intelligence concerning increased mobile flak units, the mission was flown as planned. Flak suppression missions had not been provided, and Germans exacted a heavy toll. Despite this, 70 per cent of airdropped supplies were recovered. Thirteen C-47s were shot down and17 gliders failed to make it to Bastogne. A final airdrop by 238 C-47s of the 53rd TCW later that same day had its route planned to avoid flak concentrations, and succeeded without loss.

The failure of ground forces – lacking direct radio contact with IX TCC – to report either flak sites or the location of secure corridors were among the many problems with air resupply of ground forces that became apparent in the course of *Repulse*. The Bastogne resupply effort required 927 C-47 and 61 glider sorties. Total losses were 19 C-47s.

During Christmas 1945, despite heavy wartime commitments, C-47s were still used for humanitarian airlift. This Warton-based C-47 delivered Christmas/New Years' presents, donated by USAAF personnel, to Russian labour troops – liberated slave labourers – at RAF Ford. TSgt Joseph Isby flew as navigator on this flight (*Author's Collection*)

While Operation *Repulse* was resupplying Bastogne, a battalion-sized force of the 3rd Armored Division was cut off near Marcouray, on the Bulge's northern flank. A 29 C-47 435th TCG airdrop mission on 23 December lost three aircraft to flak and missed the DZ. The following day the 438th TCG launched 36 C-47s, but despite a good drop these also missed the DZ. The unit broke out before another attempt could be launched.

The airdrops were backed up by air transport operations. On 24-25 December, the 302nd TW flew 2000 tank repair specialists and their equipment from rear area depots to the Third Army to sustain the counterattack. In early January 1945, 540 IX TCC C-47s flew the newly-arrived 17th Airborne Division from England to airfields at Reims, in France, to take part in the latter stages of the Battle of the Bulge.

VICTORY

In February 1945, total USAAF C-47/53 strength stood at 1956 aircraft in the ETO and MTO (not counting ATC and second-line aircraft such as those in base flights). This meant that there were more 'Gooney Birds' than P-51s taking part in the final victory in Europe. Following the Battle of the Bulge, the casualty evacuation mission remained key, with over 17,000 patients lifted by C-47 in January and February – half of these by the 302nd TW.

MTO OPERATIONS 1944-45

The German withdrawal from Greece led to Operation *Manna*, which saw the insertion of British paratroopers fresh from *Anvil-Dragoon*. Most of the C-47s in the MTO were concentrated for *Manna*, 11 Para airdropping unopposed over Megara airfield from eight 10th TCS C-47s and six RAF Dakotas on 12 October. They were followed by resupply airdrops on the same day, another troop drop by 40 C-47s on 14 October and one by 41 C-47s on 16 October. Twenty-four hours later, reinforcements were landed at Athens-Kalmaki airfield.

In addition to moving the Twelfth Air Force from Corsica to France and Italy, MTO-based C-47s continued flying air supply and casualty evacuation missions to the partisans. Allied air superiority meant that more sorties could be flown in daylight. In addition to the 60th TCG, the 7th, 51st and 16th TCSs each undertook tours in the Balkans from October 1944 through to VE-Day.

The Fifteenth Air Force's 1st Aircrew Rescue Unit included C-47s and parachute engineers that would jump in to prepare airstrips where shot-down aircrew could be picked up. They first went into action on the night of 2-3 August, with C-47s dropping engineers south of Belgrade and returning on the night of 9-10 August to pick up 268 personnel, 226 of them Allied aircrew.

Parachute drops in support of Italian partisans increased over the

During Operation *Manna*, external cargo was carried in British-type parapacks with Mk III containers – seen here being loaded under a C-47 by British paratroopers and 51st TCW aircrew at Foggia (*National Archives*)

This overhead view shows 51st TCW C-47s massing at Foggia in October 1944 in preparation for Operation *Manna*. The transports are taxiing past resident Fifteenth Air Force B-24s parked on their dispersal pads

winter of 1944-45, with the 64th TCG and 2641st Special Group (Provisional) carrying out the bulk of the effort by day and night. Small-scale airdrops into northern Italy took place up until war's end. For example, on 20-21 April 1945, Operation *Herring* saw 20 C-47s of the 64th TCG drop 220 Italian paratroopers behind German lines.

OPERATION *VARSITY*

In early 1945, the 52nd TCW moved forward to airfields in the Chartres area, being joined at that time by the 50th TCW, based around Amiens, and the 53rd TCW, based at airfields in the Orleans area. Only the 316th TCG remained in England. All groups were soon heavily committed to vital, but hazardous, intratheatre transport and casualty evacuation flights in winter weather.

By March the Rhine was the main barrier between the Allied armies and the German interior. The FAAA had planned since November 1944 to help breach it through an airborne assault to secure the Diersfordterwald – an area of high ground five miles east of the Rhine near Wesel. While the FAAA had continued to plan for independent strategic airborne operations, there was little confidence in this concept after Arnhem. The FAAA concept was opposed by both ground commanders (who needed the C-47s for resupply and casualty evacuation, and for the paratroopers as elite infantry) and air commanders (independent or strategic airborne operations would divert bombers away from priority targets).

Diersfordterwald would be where the 21st Army Group would stage Operation *Plunder* – its main amphibious assault. Reflecting the lesson of *Market-Garden*, Operation *Varsity's* focus was tactical, and linked to ground operations. The ten DZ/LZs were all close to their objectives, and all were concentrated in a 6x5 mile area within artillery range of the ground forces.

The 10th TCS C-47 (equipped with SCR-717C radar) that led the initial fly-in to Kalmaki airfield, in Greece, is used as a grandstand for a professional appraisal of a follow-up airdrop on 16 October 1944

Having opened the cowl flaps, two aircrew from the 10th TCS prep the engine of their C-47 before starting up for Operation *Manna*. Their flight jackets are marked with American flags – useful on forward Balkan airfields (*National Archives*)

The assault areas for Operation *Varsity* are clearly marked on this map (*Author's Collection*)

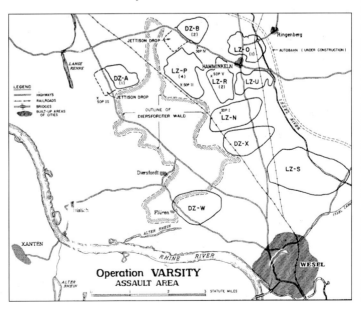

A massive, overwhelming initial air assault to break resistance was planned. The paratroopers would be dropped in daylight after the assault across the Rhine started, and pathfinders would drop with the first serials of the main force, rather than before. Because the objective was in Germany, the C-47s would encounter the massive flak defences that had been built to oppose the Allied bomber offensive – many Troop Carrier Group C-47s were modified with self-sealing tanks. Some 1264 C-47s, supplemented by 117 larger C-46s, would take part, along with almost 2000 gliders. Six-hundred C-47s (mainly from the 53rd TCW in France) would double tow CG-4As, which had never been done operationally. Twenty minutes after the last glider, 240 B-24s would airdrop supplies.

The operation was preceded by extensive training and joint exercises. The large-scale rehearsal mission Operation *Token* was flown by IX TCC C-47s, which joined up with the US 17th Airborne Divisions at airfields in France. Three 52nd TCW groups would fly from Britain, while the double-tow gliders would be among the C-47s taking off from France.

On 24 March, a few hours after *Plunder* had commenced, *Varsity* was launched. Escorted by 500 fighters, with a further 900 fighters covering the objective area, the 2046 US (and 880 RAF) transports and gliders took two-and-a-half hours to pass overhead, forming up into two columns – one for each airborne division, the British 6th and US 17th, over Wavre, near Brussels. The streams then flew on to 'Yalta', which was the codename for a checkpoint 12 miles west of the Rhine where the different serials would each turn and head for their LZ/DZs.

Flak suppression air strikes around DZs and LZs were coordinated with long-range artillery fires. The pathfinder paratroopers and C-47s led the main force, rather than preceding it. Leading the stream to the British drop was the 6th Airborne Division in C-47s of the 61st, 315th and 316th TCGs, followed by RAF transports and glider tugs. In the first wave of the 17th Airborne was the 507th PIR, led by Col Edson Raff (who had opened Operation *Torch*), and it was delivered by 298 C-47s in seven serials. They were followed by more paratroops from C-46s and C-47s and then the main glider mission – five serials of 296 C-47s with double tows to the southern US LZs – followed by 314 C-47s with single tows to the northern LZs. They were in turn followed by the low-level B-24s, some dropping as low as 100 ft. The airdrop was the most accurate of the war, with 80 per cent of supplies recovered. The paratroopers successfully linked up with ground troops on the afternoon of 24 March.

Despite these efforts, the massive flak defences were still able to inflict painful losses – 44 US transports and 15 B-24s were downed. Veteran B-24 crews were shocked by the intensity of low altitude flak, while the C-46s proved vulnerable to battle damage.

VARSITY VETERAN

2Lt Wesley M Kolbe was the pilot of C-47 41-24325 *Mary* of the 61st TCS/314th TCG during *Varsity*. His

Aircrew from the 439th TCG are briefed on the part that they will play in Operation *Varsity* at their base at Chateaudun, in France (*National Archives*)

61st TCG C-47s stand at the eastern end of the runway at Chipping Ongar on 24 March 1945, ready to accept paratroops of the British 6th Airborne Division. The latter would drop near the Wesel area of the Rhine (*National Archive via Roger Freeman*)

The 91st TCS/439th TCG gets ready at its Chateaudun base for the double tow that characterised Operation *Varsity*. This mission was the first, and only, time that C-47s double towed CG-4As operationally, although most Troops Carrier Groups had undertaken routine training with such a configuration since 1942-43 (*National Archives*)

This nylon CG-4A tow rope, with the intercom cord entwined around it, is about to be hooked up to a C-47 of the 85th TCS/437th TCG at Coulommiers, in France, prior to the aircraft participating in Operation *Varsity* (*National Archives*)

crew for this mission consisted of 2Lt Donald E Holman (co-pilot) and Cpls Cleo E Werntz (crew chief) and Philip Spitz (radio operator). Kolbe recalled;

'It was a beautifully clear morning when I taxied my C-47 "J-Jig" out onto the runway in readiness for the take-off of the impending mission, *Varsity*. All aircraft from our Airstrip B-44 (Poix, in France) were assigned the task of towing CG-4A gliders to a landing zone in enemy territory across the River Rhine.

'My aircraft was the last one of the squadron to take-off, leaving the runway behind at 0941 hrs. We got into formation at a fairly fast rate, and rendezvoused to the right. We then made a wide circle of the field to get into position, attain an altitude of 1500 ft and be back over the field at a predetermined time.

'We started out on our briefed course at approximately 1015 hrs, at which time we were in good formation. The formation on course was loose, and at times our indicated airspeed read as low as 85 mph, which in my opinion is far too slow for a C-47 with a glider in tow. At this indicated airspeed we were still gaining on the element ahead of us. To keep from overrunning, I slipped in and out of position with use of the rudder. An approach to stalling speed was noticeable several times on the way to our LZ by the shuddering of my aeroplane.

'The weather up to the west bank of the Rhine was CAVU (ceiling and visibility unlimited). The sun, added to the excitement of the mission, at times made our cockpit extremely warm. Checkpoints along the briefed route were observed, but compass beacons and the "Pundits" (a white light which flashes a double signal at intervals) were not picked up. At several other fields along the course troop carrier activity was noticeable. I assumed that this was in preparation for the "big show".

'At a position between two of our check points – "Vega" and "Kingston", about 50 miles from LZ "N", where we were to release our gliders – I observed C-46 type aircraft straggling in groups of twos and threes, and sometimes singly, away from the battle zone. At this time I started to sweat. Gathering from the manner in which they straggled out, that they must have caught hell.

'As I approached the swift-flowing Rhine, it seemed that each and all ground structures were ablaze. At this point, or shortly before, our aircraft began to pick up fighter cover, which did not attain its full strength until we reached the near bank of the river. At this time I gave the order for all crew members to don their battle equipment, as soon we were to enter hostile territory. I switched to full gas tanks, put my gear handle in neutral and put my mixture controls in emergency rich. Now our element held an indicated altitude of 1700 ft, stacked slightly higher to avoid the prop-wash of the element ahead. As I looked ahead at the rest of the formation, and the point at which we were to cross the Rhine, I saw clouds of smoke hanging above the battle area. Our fighter cover now attained full strength, and as I looked about I saw fighter aircraft (P-51s, P-47s and a few Mosquito bombers) below, above and to either side of my ship.

'A glance to the right brought relief to my mind, as I observed a formation of approximately 20 aircraft in good formation leaving the battle zone. Reasoning that this formation seemingly sustained a minimum of damage released some of the tension that had mounted with my approach to enemy territory. Our formation had now closed in, flying wing-tip to wing-tip, and from here on in to the DZ we flew a straight course (similar to a bomb-run), taking no evasive action. At 1232 hrs the Rhine passed beneath my wings, and I saw several assault boats in the process of crossing. In this same glance I took in a view of the woodlands just east of our LZ "N".

'Visibility was cut down to between one-half and one mile due to the smoke rising from the battle zone. This may have been caused, in part, to the smoke screen laid down by Field Marshal Montgomery's advancing forces. I took visual note of the apex of the "V" formed by the Diersfordter Woodland, directly en route to our LZ, which assured me that I was on course, and in a few moments our attached glider would be in free flight and handed down into the very teeth of the enemy.

'Time only allowed for momentary glances, as I was extremely

C-47 *FLAK BAIT* of the 85th TCS/437th TCG is marshalled into position so that it can be linked to two CG-4A gliders at Coulommiers just minutes before departing on a *Varsity* mission. *FLAK BAIT* has apparently been renamed, with an earlier name and personal insignia hastily painted out. Its scoreboard includes one parachute drop, two glider missions, five casualty evacuation missions and an indeterminate number of resupply missions (*National Archives*)

C-47 42-68835 *RUBY ANN* of the 72nd TCS/434th TCG was photographed in early 1945. Note the name *JAY* on the engine cowling, in addition to nose art (*Author's Collection*)

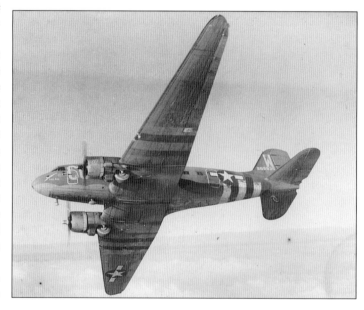

occupied keeping my aeroplane in formation, together with checking emergency precautions. I had just finished checking for what seemed the hundreth time when my ship surged ahead, indicating that the glider had released. After flying an exacting course for over two-and-a-half hours, it was a great relief that, although still over enemy territory, my mission had been completed. I need now only to guide my crew and aircraft out of this invasion area and to comparative safety west of the Rhine River. I opened the throttles wide and the aircraft leaped ahead as I started to follow the formation in a tight turn to the right.

'Looking off to the left at the ship which I was to follow in my turn, I saw a P-51 receive a direct hit and fall off on its right wing and explode. Unable to stay with my formation any longer, I steepened my bank and dove underneath the tow ropes of the aeroplanes which had been to my left (the rest of my element), and which were now above me. The steep bank to the right by our aircraft was necessary to avoid the town of Wesel, which was believed to be heavily protected by the enemy.

'In the process of returning to my formation, I looked down and saw the Rhine once more passing beneath me, across which at this time appeared to be a huge supply bridge for our advancing armies. With this came the realisation that our job was fully done, and we were back in friendly territory. I let out a yell, and vigorously slapped my co-pilot, 2Lt Donald E Hollman, on the back. I called to my crew chief and radio operator to make sure that they were okay. The radio operator's face was covered with perspiration, and with little wonder. He knew, as well as I, that our aircraft afforded little protection from enemy ground fire, especially at the extremely low airspeed and altitude we must fly on such a mission. I made a visual check of the panel instruments and all else within eye-distance of my seat. The rest of my crew made a thorough check of the aeroplane. It was after this inspection that I was reasonably certain no damage had been inflected to "Mary 325" – our aircraft.

'A Rope Drop Area had been predesignated, and it was now in full view. I gave the signal for the glider tow rope to be dropped. I now found time to remove my flak suit and battle equipment. My co-pilot did likewise. The aircraft of our squadron were once again in good formation. Looking beneath me, I observed several formations of seven and eight B-24s flying into the invaded area on a supply drop. The rest of the trip back to our home base was uneventful – except for the smiles worn by members of the ship, with a "job well done" to their credit.'

VICTORY IN EUROPE

The last days of the war included a major high-priority transport operation that involved many of the C-47s in the ETO. Air resupply to forces advancing into Germany was critical. The situation was similar to that in the advance across France, with airlifts – sometimes airdrops – being relied on to bring supplies to advancing army units that still often encountered fanatical last-ditch resistance. Former German airstrips were quickly surveyed, and C-47-towed gliders were used to insert airfield control parties and engineers to put captured airfields into operation.

The last months of the war saw many examples of how indispensable the C-47 had become. On 22 March, a 91st TCS C-47 evacuated wounded from the Remagen bridgehead by snatching up a CG-4A that

A glider snatch pick-up was used in a few high-value situations, such as the first air evacuation of wounded from the Remagen bridgehead – and was also used to recover some of the relatively few gliders retrieved intact from Normandy and the Netherlands. This photograph, taken in Germany in the spring of 1945, shows medical personnel watching from their ambulances (at a safe distance) (*National Archives*)

had previously landed and been loaded for urgent evacuation. On 9-10 April, 441st TCG airdrops – 34 and 16 sorties, respectively – near Crailsheim cost one C-47. Operations remained dangerous to the end, with C-47s encountering flak concentrations and Luftwaffe remnants daily. On 6 April 1945 alone, the 50th TCS lost five C-47s to fog-shrouded high ground.

Over 50,000 tons of fuel and 20,000 tons of supplies were airlifted into Germany in April, while casualties were evacuated out. In

April, liberated PoWs in Germany swelled the casualty evacuation total to over 2600 per day. Competing with these requirements was the need to be ready for a FAAA quick-response airborne operation to pre-empt last-ditch resistance. Several were planned, most involving the British 1st and US 13th Airborne Divisions, but these were overtaken by events.

The last months of the war were dangerous for C-47s. Capt Bob Decker of the 311th FS (then used for transport missions) ended up in a ground loop on the short, wet grass strip at Y-64, near Ober Ulm, in Germany, in April 1945. He and the co-pilot were able to feather the propeller before collapsing a main gear, which threw the left propeller into the cockpit, fortunately without killing anyone (*William Louie*)

IMMEDIATE POST-WAR OPERATIONS

VE-Day saw USAAF C-47s help airlift troops to Norway and Denmark to disarm the German forces there, and then (along with bombers) start to carry out a series of airlifts throughout Europe. US PoWs were the first, picked up from camps in eastern Germany and mostly flown to Camp Lucky Strike, near Le Havre, for shipment back to the US. Other Allied prisoners and displaced persons followed. Some Troop Carrier Groups, needed for the Pacific war soon left for the US. It was planned to keep 500 C-47s in Europe, however.

The ATC, with C-47s comprising over a third of its 3700 aircraft worldwide by mid-1945, started the European Air Transport Service (EATS), which was an ETO-wide expansion of MATS. By June 1945, major bases were established at Frankfurt-am-Main, Stockholm, Budapest and Lisbon to mesh with those pre-existing at Naples, Paris, St Eval, Prestwick and Heston.

The bulk of the USAAF in the ETO/MTO started to return home in the summer of 1945. C-47s took part in 'Homebound Airlines' on both the northern and southern transatlantic routes. The ATC was reinforced with 256 C-47s and their crews from the Troop Carrier Groups, while NATS – about half of its 400 aircraft worldwide were R4Ds on VE-Day – helped fly Navy personnel to the Pacific or home.

Photographed in Algiers in June 1945, this natural-metal C-47B of MATS/EATS was marked with the 'last four' on a coloured fin band (probably repeated on a nose diamond) and the ATC insignia on the rear cargo door. Even though glider towing was never an ATC mission, note that the streamlined tail cone has been removed (*National Archives*)

Troop Carrier Groups, unlike fighter and bomber groups, often deployed without a veteran cadre. Lacking pre-war doctrine for guidance or RAF combat experience, the role of Troop Carrier Group and Troop Carrier Squadron commanding officers – many pre-war airline pilots with reserve commissions – was critical. This photograph shows one such group CO, Col William B Whitacre (left) of the 434th TCG at Aldermaston just before take-off for Operation *Market's* initial lift on 17 September 1944. He is using a C-47 elevator as a map table to review the route with lead pilots Capts James David (centre) and Karl Kirshner (*National Archives*)

CONCLUSION

C-47 units suffered from the USAAF's failure to make them a resource priority, and from competition for resources from other theatres and services. The C-47 aircrew had to repeatedly redeem doctrinal, organisational, planning and training failures in the ETO and MTO.

Both the learning curve and the feedback loop associated with the troop carrier mission were difficult. The lack of pre-war doctrine hindered evolution. Many C-47 units and aircrew were on their first combat missions when committed to the invasions of Sicily or Normandy – both complex night operations. While the technology and tactics used had some major limitations, they required an unobtainable degree of precision to make them work.

Some planning failures – the fratricide incidents when C-47s overflew ships in *Husky II* and *Fustian* and the remote location of the DZ/LZs at Arnhem – were beyond the control of the Troop Carrier Groups. In some cases, even the best planning would not have allowed crews to find an unmarked glider release point in Operation *Ladbroke*, or unmarked DZs at night in formation without navigators while penetrating an overcast on D-Day. They were asking the impossible. To achieve at once the precision night operations RAF Bomber Command took many years to perfect.

On D-Day, IX TCC had too few pathfinders, not enough Eurekas set up on DZs and insufficient Gee sets and navigators aboard C-47s – the result of their lack of priority in resource allocation. But the RAF, with navigators and Gee, also suffered from scattering. In the skies over Europe in 1942-45, precision was seldom achievable. This is what Gen Williams realised after Sicily, but the D-Day planners and some of the paratroopers remained unaware. Yet Troop Carrier Group tactics required precision formation flying at night. After trying the impossible with these tactics at Sicily and on D-Day, they shifted to mass drops by day, made possible by Allied air superiority.

C-47 units needed to master the difficult skills of joint and coalition warfighting to a greater extent than just about any USAAF force. Separating the story of C-47s in Europe from that of the gliders they towed, the soldiers they carried into battle, the aerial evacuation missions they performed, or those of the RAF units with which their operations were invariably integrated is largely artificial. The ATC integrated service and airline crews, and they were, in turn, part of intratheatre transport in the ETO/MTO that involved all US C-47/R4D units.

The USAAF's intertheatre and intratheatre transport missions benefited from pre-war doctrine and experience (including that borrowed from the airlines) that the troop carrier missions lacked. The airline model worked for ATC. A single ETO/MTO command for transport missions and resources – Knerr's solution – was never achieved. This was seen as a failure by the USAF post-war, but centralised assets frequently proved unresponsive to those that needed them most.

A US Navy R4D, in standard Olive Drab/grey, is directed to a parking place at a stateside naval air station (*National Archives*)

The C-47 was the first to demonstrate that it is easier to have multi-mission aircraft than multi-mission aircrew or organisations. In the decades since 1945, reconciling the needs of the different missions with the heritage of both the TCC's 'hit the DZ regardless' and the ATC's more cautious yet rigorous spirit of all-weather global operations has proven a challenge for the USAF.

The importance of transport aircraft to special operations was demonstrated by C-47s in France, the Balkans and Scandinavia. Casualty evacuation saved thousands of lives. C-47 airlift made possible the operation of Allied tactical aircraft from forward airfields.

The C-47 performed well as a glider tug, but this was not an effective technological solution to a tactical problem. The transport glider's rapid extinction after 1945 underlines its nature as a wartime expedient, relying on courage and skill.

The hazards of wartime transatlantic and European flying imposed heavy costs, with C-47/R4D units ending up with lengthy Rolls of Honour. C-47s made up the vast majority of total USAAF transport losses – 682 in the ETO and 244 in the MTO. Fortunately, few C-47s were lost in air combat in the ETO/MTO. In *Market-Garden*, *Repulse*, *Varsity* and other operations, German flak inflicted damage on the low-flying, unevading C-47s that would have been unsustainable in prolonged campaigns. The massacre of C-47s off Sicily was only the most dramatic of many fratricide incidents.

Tying all these elements together is the aeroplane itself. Adaptability, reliability and ruggedness carried C-47s through a tremendous range of missions – the reason why C-47s are still operational some 60 years after VE-Day.

One of the more impressive scoreboards in the IX TCC belonged to *Lady Luck* of the 87th TCS/438th TCG – 16 casualty evacuations, four paradrops, four para resupplies, five glider tows, 190 resupply and 21 PoW evacuation missions. While the total of 240 missions is a high one, the proportion of the different types reflects that IX TCC was often called on for intratheatre resupply, and only rarely to drop paratroops (*National Archives*)

APPENDICES

APPENDIX 1

C-47/R4D UNITS IN THE ETO/MTO TO VE-DAY

(All locations in the UK unless stated otherwise)

AIR TRANSPORT COMMAND

ATC reported directly to HQ USAAF. ATC Wings were administrative rather than operational units, and did not have subordinate groups and squadrons of aircraft. Each wing was responsible for a number of bases, ground units and aircraft – mainly C-47s – for intratheatre transport, and for providing support for intertheatre transport and ferry missions

Air Transport Command, European Wing
Formed: 1/43
Headquarters: Prestwick

Air Transport Command, North Atlantic Wing
Formed: 6/42
Headquarters: Presque Isle, ME

Air Transport Command, Africa and Middle East Wing
Formed: 6/42 and dissolved into two wings 6/43
Headquarters: Cairo, Egypt

Air Transport Command, Middle East Wing
Formed: 6/43
Headquarters: Cairo, Egypt

Air Transport Command, Central Africa Wing
Formed: 6/43.
Headquarters: Khartoum, Sudan

MAJOR HEADQUARTERS ETO/MTO

US Strategic Air Forces
(Parent Command of the Eighth, Ninth and Fifteenth Air Forces, formed 1/44) Direct-reporting units included C-47-equipped 302nd Transport Wing 9/44-5/45

Mediterranean Allied Tactical Air Forces
(Parent Command of the Twelfth Air Force and RAF Desert Air Force) Direct-reporting units included C-47-equipped 51st Troop Carrier Wing 8/44-5/45

IX Troop Carrier Command
Under Ninth Air Force 10/43-7/44 (but operationally under direct command of Allied Expeditionary Air Forces 12/43-7/44). HQ used for (and aircraft part of) Provisional Troop Carrier Air Division (PTCAD), along with 51st TCW (MATAF) 7-8/44, First Allied Airborne Army (FAAA) 8/44-5/45
Components: 50th TCW (43-45), 52nd TCW (8/44-5/45), 53rd TCW (44-45), Pathfinder School/Group (43-45). As PTCAD, 51st TCW (7/44-8/44)
Formed: 10/43, Cottesmore (From I TCC, XII TCC, VIII ASC and IX AFSC elements), but slowly built up and not fully operational until 2/44
Location: Cottesmore (10-12/43), St Vincent's, Grantham (12/43-9/44), Sunninghill Park, Ascot (co-located with FAAA, IX TCC CP at Eastecote Place, Uxbridge) (9/44-5/45)
IX Troop Carrier Command also included C-47/53-equipped headquarters detachment (three of which detached to Rome, Italy, 7-8/44)

NORTHWEST AFRICA AIR FORCES/XII TROOP CARRIER COMMAND (PROVISIONAL)

Formed 21/3/43. Command headquarters for USAAF TCWs (plus 316th TCG) in MTO. Also referred to as II TCC. Cut back 12/43, disbanded 2/44

Middle East Air Forces
Became Ninth Air Force 12/42

VIII Air Support Command
Was to have commanded ETO TCWs before IX TCC established. Had provisional TCC HQ that was incorporated into IX TCC

VIII Air Force Service Command
Parent organisation of all Eighth Air Force support functions, including some flying units equipped with C-47s

IX Air Force Service Command
(Redesignated from IX ASC 1/44)
Parent organisation of all Ninth Air Force support functions, including some equipped with C-47s

Northwest Africa Air Forces/XII Air Force Service Command
Parent organisation of Twelfth Air Force support functions

Balkan Air Forces
USAAF/RAF operational command of C-47 squadrons detached for Balkan special operational duties

TROOP CARRIER WINGS

50th TCW

Component Groups: 315th TCG (9/43-2/44), 434th TCG (10/43-5/44), 436th TCG (11/42-2/44), 439th TCG (5/44-5/45), 440th TCG (4/44-5/45), 441st TCG (4/44-5/45), 442nd TCG (3/44-5/45)

Formed: 1/41 Wright, OH (as 50th Transport Wing, re-designated 50th TCW 7/42). Functioned as training and transport unit until moving overseas

Location: Wright, OH (1-5/42), Camp Williams WI (5-9/42), Knobnoster MO (9/42-4/43), Camp Mackall NC (4-7/43), Pope NC (7-9/43), Cottesmore (7-11/43), Bottesford (11/43-4/44), Exeter (4-10/44), Le Mans, France (10-11/44), Chartres, France (11/44-5/45)

Subordinated to: I TCC (7/42-9/43), IX TCC (9/43-5/45)

Elements of HQ detached to Italy 7-8/44. Provisional TCG HQ formed during detachments to Italy for *Anvil-Dragoon* 7-8/44

51st TCW

Component Groups: 60th TCG (9/42-5/45), 61st TCG, (9/42-2/44), 62nd TCG (42-45), 64th TCG (42-45)

Formed: Pope NC (6/42) as 51st TW, redesignated TCW (7/42)

Location: Pope NC (6-7/42), Greenham Common (9-11/42), Algiers, Algeria (11/42-3/43), La Senia, Algeria (3-5/43), Mascara, Algeria (5-6/43), Gourbrine, Tunisia (6-8/43), Gela, Sicily (8-9/43), Catania, Sicily (9/43-6/44), Lido di Roma, Italy (6/44-1/45), Siena, Italy (1/45-5/45)

Subordinated to: Eighth Air Force (6-9/42), Twelfth Air Force (9/42-1/43), XII Air Force Service Command (1-6/43), NW African AF TCC (7-9/43), XII TCC (10-11/43), MATAF (12/43-8/44), PTCAD (8/44) Twelfth Air Force/Mediterranean Allied Tactical Air Forces (8/44-5/45)

52nd TCW

Component Groups: 61st TCG (2/44-5/45), 313th TCG (5/43-5/45), 314th TCG (5/43-5/45), 315th TCG (2/44-5/45), 316th TCG (2/44-5/45)

Formed: Daniel GA (6/42) as 52nd TW, redesignated TCW (7/42)

Location: Daniel GA (6-7/42), Bowman KY (7-8/42), Pope NC (8/42-4/43), Oujda, Morocco (5-7/43), Kairouan, Tunisia (7-9/43), Agrigento, Sicily (9/43-2/44), Exton Hall, Cottesmore (2/44-3/45), Amiens, France (3-5/45)

Subordinated to: XII Air Force Service Command (1-6/43), NW African AF TCC (7-9/43), XII TCC (10-11/43), Twelfth Air Force (12/43-2/44), IX TCC (2-8/44), PTCAD (8/44), IX TCC (8/44-5/45)

315th TCG operationally attached 8/43-2/44

53rd TCW

Component Groups: 434th TCG (5/44-5/45), 435th TCG (2/44-5/45), 436th TCG (2/44-5/45), 437th TCG (3/44-5/45), 438th TCG (2/44-5/45), 439th TCG (2-5/44)

Formed: Milwaukee WI (8/42)

Location: Pope NC (8-9/42), Ft Sam, Houston TX (9-11/42), Bergstrom TX (11/42-4/43), Sedalia MO (4-9/43), Maxton NC (9-12/43), Pope NC (12/43-1/44), Bowdon House, Greenham Common (2/44-2/45), Voisenon, France (2-5/45)

Subordinated to: IX TCC/PTCAD (2/43-5/45)

Headquarters detached to Tarquina, Italy 7-8/44, leaving provisional TCG behind in UK

TRANSPORT AND SPECIAL OPERATIONS WINGS, GROUPS AND UNITS

302nd Transport Wing

Component Groups: 27th TG (9/44-5/45), 31st TG (9/44-5/45)

Activated: 9/44, Grove

Subordinated to: USSTAF (44-45) (but remained integrated with the Eighth Air Force for support and logistics)

Base: Grove (9/44-5/45)

IXth Troop Carrier Command Service Wing (Provisional)

Activated: 4/44, Charmy Down

Subordinated to: IX TCC (4/44-5/45)

Bases: Charmy Down (4/44-9/44), North Witham (9/44-5/45)

Used to support TCGs based in France from depots in Britain. Also used for special operations. Used borrowed C-47s from TCGs, supplemented with its own (often 'war weary') C-47s, C-46s, C-109s and other aircraft

1st TG (Provisional)

Component Squadrons: 315th TS (9/44-5/45), 325th FS (10/44-5/45), 326th FS (9-10/44)

Activated: 9/44 Grove

Subordinated to: IX AFSC (9/44-5/45)

Bases: Grove (9/44), Creil, France (9/44-5/45)

Changes: Formed with 24 C-47s (plus 24 C-46s coming from US), 10 UC-64s

Eighth Air Force Ferry and Transport Command

Activated: 7/42

Component Squadrons: 86th TS (7/42-4/43), 87th TS (42-4/43)

Subordinated to: Air Section, VIII Air Force Service Command

Bases: Hendon

Changes: Incorporated into 27th TG 4/43. Started off with ex-RAF and light aircraft, operating C-47s by 8/42

27th TG

Component Squadrons: 86th TS (4/43-5/45), 87th TS (4/43-11/44), 320th TS (11/43-5/45), 321st TS (11/43-5/45), 310th FS (11/43-11/44), 311th FS (11/43-4/45), 312th FS (11/43-11/44), 325th FS (11/43-12/44), 2920th FS (Provisional) (44-45)

Activated: Meadowbank, London (4/43)

Subordinated to: VIII AFSC (4/43-2/44), USSTAF (2-9/44) (but remained integrated with the Eighth Air Force for support and logistics), 302nd TW (9/44-5/45)

Bases: Warton (4/43-9/44) (during this time 86th TS was Northolt based, 87th TS Warton, 320th TS Honington, 321st TS Langford Lodge, HQ Meadowbank, Le Bourget, France (9/44-2/45) (321st TS moved to Grove 9/44, Villacoublay, France (2/45-5/45). 310 FS based Chartres, France (7-11/44)

Changes: Included multiple types. 310th FS resubordinated to 31st TG 11/44. 311th FS transitioned to transport mission with C-47s 7-8/44, detachment to Istres, under operational control of 1 ATAF (9/44-3/45), then directly subordinated to 302nd TW (4/45). 87th TS detached to Chipping Ongar for petrol lift duties 10/44, then resubordinated to Base Air Depot Area of VIII AFSC 11/44 at Grove, then to 31st TG after a month. 312th FS at Langford Lodge to 8/44, then moved to Warton and transferred to Grove 9/44. 320th TS detachment at Le Bourget (at first with 20 UC-64s, then replaced with C-47s) (9/44). Detachments at Northolt and in Sweden, 1944-45. Also responsible for operating VIP aircraft for US and British high command

31st TG

Component Squadrons: 87th TS (12/44-5/45), 313th TS (10/43-5/45), 314th TS (10/43-5/45), 315th TS (11/43-9/44), 310th FS (11/44-4/45), 312th FS/TS (9/44-5/44), 326th FS (7/43-9/44), 326th FS (12/44-5/45)
Activated: Bushy Park (7/43)
Subordinated to: IX AFSC (7/43-8/44), 302nd TW (8/44-5/45)
Bases: Bushy Park (7-10/43), Grove (10/43-9/44). Dispersed by squadron – Bolleville-La Haye du Puit, France (313th TS), Maupertus, France (314th TS), HQ and remainder at Querqueville, France (9/44-11/44), Chartres, France (11-12/44), Grove (12/44-5/45) – 310th FS to Grove 11/44
Changes: Included multiple aircraft types. Formed with 20 C-47s, 6 UC-64. C-46s added early 1945. Detachments at Northolt and Harrowbeer mid-44. 326th FS directly under IX AFSC 9/44-5/45. 310th FS resubordinated to direct 302nd TW command 4/45. 312th FS (also referred to as 312th TS) at Grove from 9/44

810th Provisional Bomb Group/492nd Bomb Group

Subordinated to: Eighth Air Force (administrative), OSS (operational)
Bases: Alconbury (11/43-2/44), Watton (2-8/44), Harrington (8/44-5/45)
Changes: Redesignated 492nd BG (8/44). Eighth AF 'Carpetbaggers' used for special operations. Mainly equipped with modified B-24s, but also 4-5 C-47s (in 7-8/44), Mosquitos, A-26s and other types. C-47s concentrated in 856th BS 10/44-5/45, with three other squadrons used for bombing missions. Previously, unit had consisted of 36th and 406th BS and (from May 44) 788th and 866th BS

15th/2641st Special Group (Provisional)

Activated: 1/45, Italy
Subordinated to: MASAF (1/45-3/45), MATAF (3-5/45)
Bases: Brindisi, Italy
Changes: Redesignated 2641st Special Group 3/45. Used for special operations in Italy and the Balkans. Group primarily equipped with modified B-24s

1st Aircrew Rescue Unit

Components: 4 C-47s
Activated: Foggia/Brindisi, 1944
Subordinated to: 15th Air Force
Bases: Brindisi, Foggia, Italy
Changes: Used to parachute in engineers and medical personnel and fly shot-down aircrew out of the Balkans

Service Group/Base/Tactical/Sub Air Deport and Base Flights

Activated: 1942-45
Subordinated to: Service Groups, depots, sub-depots and airfields throughout the ETO/MTO
Changes: These flights mainly used smaller aircraft, but increasingly used one or a few C-47s (often overhauled TCC aircraft) to fly supplies and technicians to forward based or to force-landed aircraft

TROOP CARRIER GROUPS AND SQUADRONS (All designated transport prior to 7/42)

50th Provisional TCG

Also referred to as Detachment 'A'. Made up of air elements of the 50th TCW that did not deploy to Italy for *Anvil-Dragoon* (7-8/44), remaining in England and France

53rd Provisional TCG

Details as 50th

60th TCG

Component Squadrons: 10th TCS (40-45), 11th TCS (40-45), 12th TCS (40-45) (detached for special operations at various times in 1944), 28th TCS (42-45)
Activated: Olmstead PA (12/40)
Subordinated to: Eighth AFSC (6-8/42), 51st TCW (9/42-5/45)
Bases: Westover MA (5/41-6/42), Chelveston (6/42-8/42), Aldermaston (8/42-11/42), Portreath (11/42), Tafaraoui, Algeria (11/42), Relizane, Algeria (11/42-5/43), Thiersville, Algeria (5-6/43), El Djem, Tunisia (6-8/43), Gela, Sicily (8-10/43), Gebrini, Sicily (10/43-3/44), Brindisi, Italy (3-10/44), Pomigliano, Italy (10/44-5/45)
The group eventually took over special operations commitment from 62nd TCG 3-10/44

61st TCG

Component Squadrons: 13th TCS (40-42), 14th TCS (40-45), 15th TCS (40-45), 53rd TCS (42-45), 59th TCS (42-45)
Activated: Olmstead PA (12/40)
Subordinated to: Eighth AF (6-9/42), 51st TCW (9/42-2/44), 52nd TCW (2/44-5/45)
Bases: Olmstead PA (12/40-7/41), Augusta GA (7/41-5/42), Pope NC, (5-9/42), Lubbock TX (9/42-2/43), Pope NC (2/43-5/43), Lourmel, Morocco (5-6/43), Kairouan, Tunisia (6-9/43), Licata, Sicily (9-10/43), Sciacca, Sicily (10/43-2/44), Barkston Heath (2/44-3/45), Abbeville, France (3-4/45)
Operated from Chipping Ongar for *Varsity*

62nd TCG

Component Squadrons: 4th TCS (40-45), 7th TCS (40-45), 8th TCS (40-45), 51st TCS (40-45)
Activated: McClellan CA (12/40)
Subordinated to: Eighth AF (9/42), 51st TCW (9/42-5/45)
Bases: McClellan CA (12/40-5/42), Kellogg MI (5-7/42), Florence SC (7-8/42), Keevil (9-11/42), Tafaraoui, Algeria (11-12/42), Nouvion, Algeria (12/42-5/43), Matemore, Algeria (5-7/43), Kairouan, Tunisia (7-9/43), Ponte Olivo, Sicily (9/43-2/44), Brindisi, Italy (2-3/44), Ponte Olivo, Sicily (2-5/44), Gaudo, Italy (5-6/44), Galera, Italy (6-9/44), Malignano, Italy (9/44-1/45), Tarquina, Italy (1-5/45)
Changes: 4th TCS detached to CBI 4-7/44. Frequent detachments of squadrons to special operations. First such detachment was 8th TCS to Gioia del Colle 11/43-2/44, replaced by 7th and 51st TCS at Brindisi 2-3/44. 7th detached to Brindisi for special operations to Balkans 10-12/44, then detached to Tarquina for special operations to northern Italy 12/44-1/45. 4th and 8th TCS detached to Siena-Malignan for special operations 1-2/45. 51st TCS detached to Brindisi for special operations 10/44-3/45

64th TCG

Component Squadrons: 4th TCS (4/44-6/44) (attached), 16th TCS (40-45), 17th TCS (40-45), 18th TCS (40-45), 35th TCS (6/42-45), 54th TCS (6/42)
Activated: Duncan TX (12/40) (using 3rd, 4th & 7th TS as a cadre)
Subordinated to: Eighth AF (6-9/42), 51st TCW (9/42-5/45). Detached to CBI (4-7/44)
Bases: Duncan TX (12/40-7/41), March CA (7/41-2/42), Hamilton CA (2-7/42), Ramsbury (8/42-11/42), Blida, Algeria (12/42-6/43), Kairouan, Tunisia (6-7/43), El Djem, Tunisia (7/43-8/43), Comiso, Sicily (8/43-4/44 (rear HQ to 7/44), Rome-Ciampino, Italy (7/44-1/45), Rosignano, Italy (1-5/45). 35th TCS detached to Telegema, Algeria 1-3/43. 18th TCS detached to Tripoli, Libya 3-4/43. 18th and 35th TCS detached to Oujda, Morocco, 11-12/43. 18th TCS detached to Brindisi, Italy, for special operations 1-5/44. Air echelon detached to Istres, France 9-11/44. 16th TCS detached to Brindisi, Italy, for special operations 3-5/45

313th TCG

Component Squadrons: 29th TCS (42-45), 47th TCS (42-45), 48th TCS (42-45), 49th TCS (42-45)

Activated: Daniel GA (3/42)

Subordinated to: I TCC (7/42-4/43), 52nd TCW (5/43-5/45)

Bases: Daniel GA (3-6/42), Bowman KY (6-8/42), Florence SC (8-12/42), Maxton NC (12/42-4/43), Oujda, Morrocco (5-6/43), Kairouan, Tunisia (6-8/43), Sciacca, Sicily (8-10/43), Trapani-Milo, Sicily (10/43-2/44), Folkingham (2/44-2/45), Achiet, France (2/45-5/45)

Changes: HQ moved to England 2/44, rest of group followed 3/44. First C-46s arrived 1/45. Re-equipped with 90 C-46s by *Varsity* (first TCG in ETO to re-equip)

314th TCG

Component Squadrons: 30th TCS (42), 31st TCS (42), 32nd TCS (42-45), 50th TCS (42-45), 61st TCS (43-45), 62nd TCS (43-45)

Activated: 3/42 Drew FL

Subordinated to: I TCC (7/42-5/43), 52nd TCW (5/43-5/45)

Bases: Drew FL (3-6/42), Bowman KY (6-11/42), Knobnoster MO (11/42-2/43), Lawson GA (2-5/43), Berguent, Morocco (5-6/43), Kairouan, Tunisia (6-8/43), Castelvetrano, Sicily (8/43-2/44), Saltby (2/44-2/45), Poix, France (2-5/45)

315th TCG

Component Squadrons: 33rd TCS (42), 34th TCS (42-45) (largely flew scheduled flights for MATS 5/43-2/44), 35th TCS (2-6/42), 43rd TCS (42-45) (attached to NW Africa Air Service Command 5/43-2/44), 54th TCS (6/42), 309th TCS (10/43-5/45), 310th TCS (10/43-5/45)

Activated: Olmstead PA (2/42)

Subordinated to: Eighth AF ASC (12/42-9/43), 50th TCW (9/43-2/44), 52nd TCW (2/44-5/45)

Bases: Olmstead PA (2-6/42), Bowman KY (6-8/42), Florence SC (8-10/42), Northern Route-Greenland (ASR duties) (10-12/42), Aldermaston (12/42-11/43), Welford (11/43-2/44), Spanhoe (2/44-4/45), Amiens, France (4-5/45)

Changes: Deployed to UK 12/42 with 34th (C-53s) and 43rd (C-47s) TCS only. These two squadrons, with 21 aircraft, sent to North Africa 5/43 for transport duties. Reinforced to 26 aircraft each with TCG cast-offs. Returned 2-3/44. About 5-10 C-47s remained in UK 5/43-3/44, most then transferred to other units 3/44. 309th and 310th TCS arrived without aircraft, brought up to strength with replacements and 26 C-47s (and veteran crews) from 60th and 62nd TCGs 3/44. Required extensive airdrop training in UK 3-6/44 due to previous use in transport mission. Operated from Boreham for *Varsity*

316th TCG

Component Squadrons: 36th TCS (42-45), 37th TCS (42-45) (det to Ninth AF 5-9/43), 44th TCS (42-45) (added 6/42), 45th TCS (42-45) (added 6/42, based Ismailia 11/42)

Activated: Patterson OH 2/42

Subordinated to: US MEAAF (11-12/42), Ninth AF (12/42-8/43), XII TCC (attached to 52nd TCW) (8/43-2/44), 52nd TCW (2/44-5/45)

Bases: Patterson OH (2-6/42), Bowman KY (6-8/42), Del Valle TX (8-9/42), Deversoir, Egypt (11-12/42), El Adem, Libya (12/42-5/43), Nouvion, Algeria (5/43-6/43), Enfidaville, Tunisia (6/43-9/43), Maxxara, Sicily (9/43-11/43), Borizza, Sicily (11/43-2/44), Cottesmore (2/44-5/45)

Changes: Operated from Greenham Common 7-8/44 and from Weatherfield for *Varsity*. 44th and 45th TCS detached for missions in Belgian Congo 11/42

349th TCG

Component Squadrons: 23rd TCS (44-45), 311th TCS (11/43-12/44), 312th TCS (43-45), 313th TCS (43-45), 314th TCS (43-45)

Activated: Sedalia MO 11/43

Subordinated to: I TCC (11/43-3/45), 52 TCW (3-/45)

Bases: Sedalia MO (11/43-1/44), Alliance NB (1-3/44), Pope NC (3/44-3/45), Baer IN (3/45), Barkston Heath (3/45), Roye/Amy, France (4-5/45)

Changes: Used for stateside TCG (as Replacement Training Unit and Operational Training Unit) and airborne training. Deployment delayed when trained aircrew sent to IX TCC pre-D-Day. Re-equipped with C-46s before deploying to England. Carried 1st Airborne Division to Norway starting VE-Day. Used some C-47s post VE-Day. 311th TCS kept in US after receiving C-46s, deployed to Seventh Air Force

434th TCG

Component Squadrons: 71st TCS (43-45), 72nd TCS (43-45), 73rd TCS (43-45), 74th TCS (43-45)

Activated: 2/43, Alliance NB

Subordinated to: I TCC (2/43-10/43), VIIIth ASC (10/43-2/43), 50th TCW (2-5/44), 53rd TCW (5/44-5/45)

Bases: Alliance NB (2-9/43), Baer IN (5-10/43), Fulbeck (10-12/43), Welford Park (aircraft detached, HQ remains Fulbeck) (12/43-1/44), Fulbeck (1/44-3/44), Aldermaston (3/44-2/45), Mourmelon-le-Grand, France (2-5/45). Air echelon operated from Ramsbury 12/43-1/44

435th TCG

Component Squadrons : 75th TCS (43-45), 76th TCS (43-45), 77th TCS (43-45), 78th TCS (43-45)

Activated: 2/43, Bowman KY

Subordinated to: I TCC (2-10/43), 50th TCW (11/43-1/43), 53rd TCW (1/43-5/45)

Bases: Bowman KY (2-5/43), Sedalia MO (5-7/43), Pope NC (7-10/43) Baer IN (10/43), Langar (11/43-1/44), Welford Park (1/44-2/45), Bretigny, France (2-5/45)

Changes: Air echelon operated from Ramsbury 12/43-1/44. Detachment to Taquina, Italy 7-8/44

436th TCG

Component Squadrons: 79th TCS (43-45), 80th TCS (43-45), 81st TCS (43-45), 82nd TCS (43-45)

Activated: Baer IN 4/43

Subordinated to: I TCC (4/43-11/43), 50th TCW (11/43-2/44), 53rd TCW (2/44-5/45)

Bases: Baer IN (4-5/43), Alliance NB (5-8/43), Maxton NC (8-12/43), Baer IN (12/43), Bottesford (1-3/44), Membury (3/44-2/45), Melun, France (2/45-5/45)

Changes: Detachment to Voltone, Italy 7-8/44

437th TCG

Component Squadrons: 83rd TCS (43-45), 84th TCS (43-45), 85th TCS (43-45), 86th TCS (43/45)

Activated: 5/43 Baer IN

Subordinated to: I TCC (6/43-2/44), 53rd TCW (3/44-5/45)

Bases: Baer (5-6/43), Sedalia MO (6-10/43), Pope NC (10-12/43), Baer IN (12/43-1/44), Balderton (1-2/44), Ramsbury (3/44-2/45), Coulommiers-Voisins, France (2-5/45)

Changes: Detachment to Montala, Italy 7-8/44

438th TCG

Component Squadrons: 87th TCS (43-45), 88th TCS (43-45), 89th TCS (43-45), 90th TCS (43-45)

Activated: 6/43 Baer IN

Subordinated to: I TCC (6/43-1/44), 53rd TCW (2/44-5/45)

Bases: Baer IN (6/43), Sedalia MO (6-10/43), Maxton NC (10/43-1/44), Baer IN (1-2/44), Langar (2-3/44), Greenham Common (3/44-2/45), Prosnes, France (2-5/45), Amiens-Glisy, France (5/45)

Changes: Detachment to Canino Italy 7-8/44. 90th TCS operated from Welford 7-8/44

439th TCG

Component Squadrons: 91st TCS (43-45), 92nd TCS (43-45), 93rd TCS (43-45), 94th TCS (43-45)

Activated: Alliance NB 6/43

Subordinated to: I TCC (6-43/1/44), 53rd TCW (2/44-5/44), 50th TCW (5/44-5/45)

Bases: Alliance NB (6/43), Sedalia MO (6-8/43), Alliance NB (8-12/43), Maxton NC (12/43-2/44), Baer IN (2/44), Balderton (2-4/44), Upottery (4-9/44), Juvincourt, France (9/44), Lonray, France (9-11/44), Chateaudun, France (11/44-5/45)

Changes: Detachment to Orbetollo, Italy 7-8/44. During this time 93rd TCS operated from Ramsbury and Membury. Operated from Balderton for part of *Market-Garden.* 93rd TCS detached to Istres, France 11-12/44. Partially re-equipped with C-46s in 1945 after VE-Day

440th TCG

Component Squadrons: 95th TCS (43-45), 96th TCS (43-45), 97th TCS (43-45), 98th TCS (43-45)

Activated: 7/43 Baer IN

Subordinated To: I TCC (7/43-2/44), 50th TCW (4/44-5/45)

Bases: Baer IN (7/43), Sedalia MO (7-9/43), Alliance NB (7/43-1/44), Pope NC (1-2/44), Baer IN (2/44), Bottesford (3-4/44), Exeter (4-9/44), Reims, France (9/44), Le Mans, France (9-11/44), Orleans, France (11/44-5/5)

Changes: Detachment to Ombrone, Italy 7-8/44. 98th TCS operated from Ramsbury 8/44. Operated from Fulbeck in *Market-Garden*

441st TCG

Component Squadrons: 99th TCS (43-45), 100th TCS (43-45), 301st TCS (43-45), 302nd TCS (43-45)

Activated: 8/43 Sedalia MO

Subordinated To: I TCC (8/43-3/44), 50th TCW (4/44-5/45)

Bases: Sedalia (8/43-1/44), Mackall NC (1-2/44), Langar (3-4/44), Merryfield (4-9/44), Villeneuve-Vetrus, France (9-10/44), St Marceau, France (10-11/44), Dreux, France (11/44-5/45)

Changes: Detachment to Grosseto, Italy 7-8/44. During this time 301st TCS operated from Ramsbury. Operated from Langar in *Market-Garden*

442nd TCG

Component Squadrons: 303rd TCS (43-45), 304th TCS (43-45), 305th TCS (43-45), 306th TCS (43-45)

Activated: Sedalia MO, 9/43

Subordinated to: I TCC (9-43-3/44), 50th TCW (3/44-5/45)

Bases: Sedalia MO, (8-12/43), Alliance NB (12/43-1/44), Baer IN (3/44), Fulbeck (3-6/44), Weston Zoyland (6-10/44), Bonnertable/Peray, France (10-11/44), St-Andre-de-L'Eure, France (11/44-5/45)

Changes: Did not received C-47s until 12/43, training on smaller transports. Last TCG to deploy pre-D-Day, arrived in England lacking airdrop training and understrength. Detachment to Follonica, Italy 7-8/44. During this time 306th TCS operated from Ramsbury. Operated from Chilbolton during *Market-Garden*

IX TCC Pathfinder School/Group (Provisional)

Component Squadrons: 1st PF Sqn, 2nd PF Sqn, 3rd PF Sqn, 4th PF Sqn (all 44-45)

Activated: 2/44, Cottesmore with 7 C-47s

Subordinated to: IX TCC

Bases: Cottesmore (2-3/44), North Witham (3/44-9/44), Chalgrove (9/44-3/45), Chartes, France (3/45-4/45)

Changes: Gee training started Bottesford 1/44 with 2 C-47s. Detachment of 12 C-47s and crews to Marcigliano-Rome, Italy 7-8/44 under PTCAD. Redesignated 9/44, with 64 C-47s and crews. Disbanded 3-4/45, assets going to other TCGs. Training role included operational casualty evacuation and transport missions

---

US NAVY

NATS squadrons were administrative rather than operational units, hence they tended to be larger than most USAAF squadrons. Unlike USAAF C-47s, NATS R4Ds were based remotely from squadron HQ

VR-1

Activated: Norfolk (1/42)

Subordinated to: NATS (7/42-3/43), Air Transport Squadrons Atlantic Wing (3-10/43), Commander NATS Atlantic (10/43-5/45)

Home Base: Norfolk (1/42-7/43), Patuxtent River 7/43-5/45)

Mission: Atlantic Fleet support (1/42-4/43), North Atlantic route support (4/43-5/45)

Changes: Operated R5Ds as well, starting 3/43

VR-7

Activated: Miami (4/43)

Subordinated to: Air Transport Squadrons Atlantic Wing (4-10/43), Commander NATS Atlantic (10/43-5/45)

Home Base: Miami (4/43-5/45)

Mission: South Atlantic route/Caribbean support (4/43-5/45)

Headquarters Squadron, Fleet Air Wing 7

Dunkeswell (11/42-5/45)

Det To Upottery (11/44-5/45)

Mission: Support of USN in UK/Northern Europe

Operated a small number of R4Ds, in addition to other aircraft

Headquarters Squadron, Fleet Air Wing 15

Port Lyautey, Morocco (circa 3/43-5/45)

Mission: Support of USN in North Africa/Mediteranean

Operated a small number of R4Ds, in addition to other aircraft

Headquarters Flight

Hendon (circa 1/44-5/45)

Mission: Intratheatre transport – met incoming NATS R5Ds for priority shipments

Operated several R4D/C-47s (including overhauled ex-IX TCC aircraft), in addition to other aircraft

APPENDIX 2

ETO SQUADRON CODES

Most C-47s based in the ETO carried a two-digit unit code on the forward fuselage and an individual aircraft letter (or number or two-digit combination) on the after fuselage (or fin). ATC and MTO-based units did not receive these codes, instead often having an individual letter on the fin or fuselage and/or a three-digit aircraft number on the forward fuselage (or in a nose marking, originally used by ATC to identify C-47s parked on crowded aprons, and later adopted by TCGs). The 37th TG had a circular nose marking and the 31st TG a triangle, usually in white. Some MTO units used bomber-inspired fin markings (e.g., triangle M, triangle W). Some TCGs (most notably the 316th) used both codes and aircraft numbers when in IX TCC. Transport unit codes were unofficial, and subject to variation.

Other distinguishing insignia included the 27th TG fin-top flash and 31st TG fin insignia. Transport squadrons were often (but not always) distinguished by fin and nacelle markings. ATC C-47s often (but not always) wore their ATC markings on the fuselage. Some units (most notably the 86th TS in the ETO and the 12th TCS in the MTO) used elaborate squadron nose or upper fuselage insignias in 1944-45. Other units had smaller versions on fins.

In application, codes varied in colour (usually light grey) and size (30-48 inches, varying in the same squadron). All codes are for TCSs, unless otherwise noted.

2L	302nd		E5	62nd
2R	50th		H2	49th
3A	53rd		IB	77th
3B	93rd		ID	74th
3D	82nd		IH	1st Pathfinder (and Group/School aircraft)
3F	313th		J7	303rd
3I	14th		J8	92nd
3J	99th		L4	91st
3X	87th		LY	314th
4A	310th		M2	88th
4C	36th and 44th		M6	309th
4J	305th		N3	47th
4U	89th		NM	34th (usually painted in yellow)
5K	86th		Px	312th FS (used multiple second letters to identify aircraft)
5X	48th, 29th		Q7	90th
6E	44th, 36th		Q8	23rd
6Z	96th		Q9	61st
7D	80th		S2	32nd
7H	306th		S6	79th
8C	100th		SH	75th (pre-D-Day)
8Y	98th		Sx	311th FS (used multiple second letters to identify aircraft)
9E	312th TS		T2	83rd
9O	85th		T3	45th
9X	95th		Tx	86th TS (used multiple second letters to identify aircraft)
AP	1st Pathfinder(?)		U5	81st
BP	2nd Pathfinder(?)		UA	43rd (usually painted in yellow)
Cx	321st TS (used multiple second letters to identify aircraft)		V4	304th
CJ	71st		Y9	15th
CK	75th (post D-Day)		Wx	HQ, 27th TG (used multiple second letters to identify aircraft)
CM	78th		W6	97th
CN	73rd		W7	37th
CP	3rd Pathfinder(?)		X5	59th
CU	72nd		Z4	301st
CW	76th		Z7	29th
D8	94th		Z8	84th

All scale drawings are of a Douglas C-47A, and are to 1/96th scale

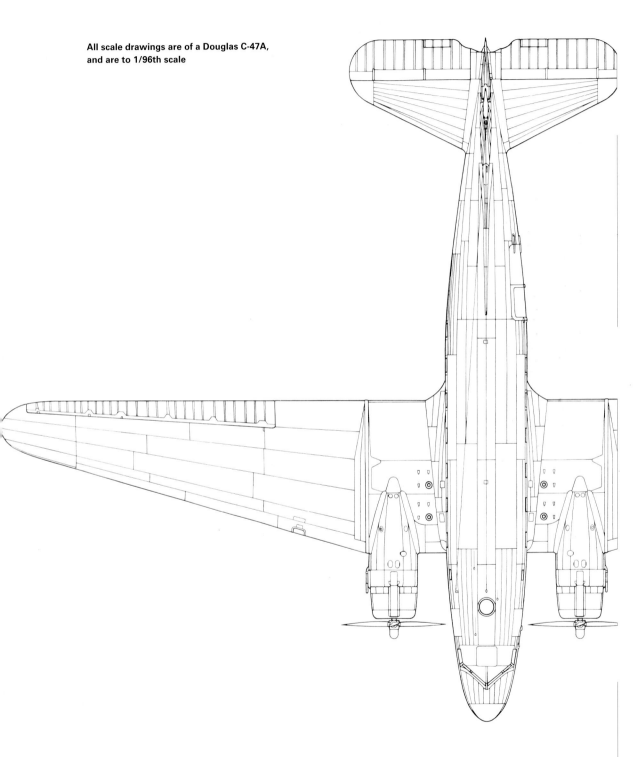

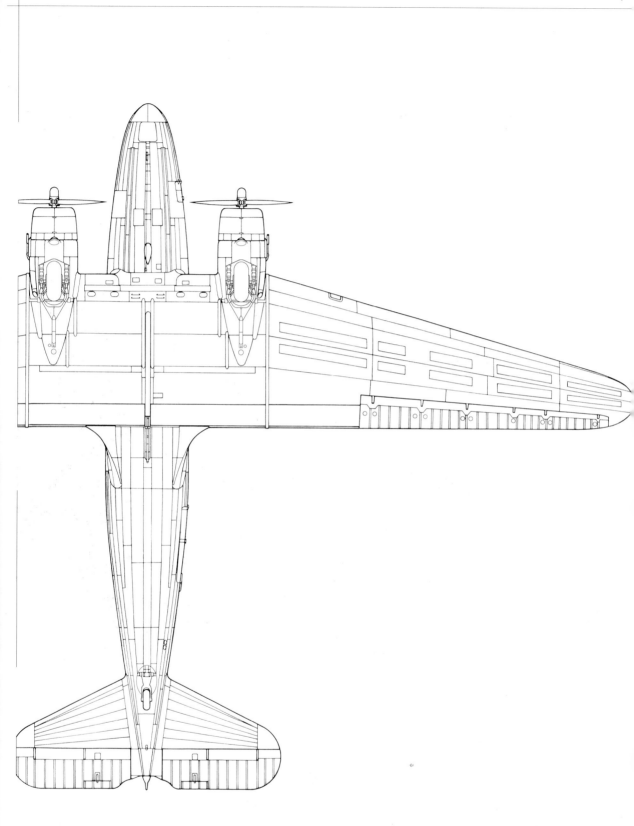

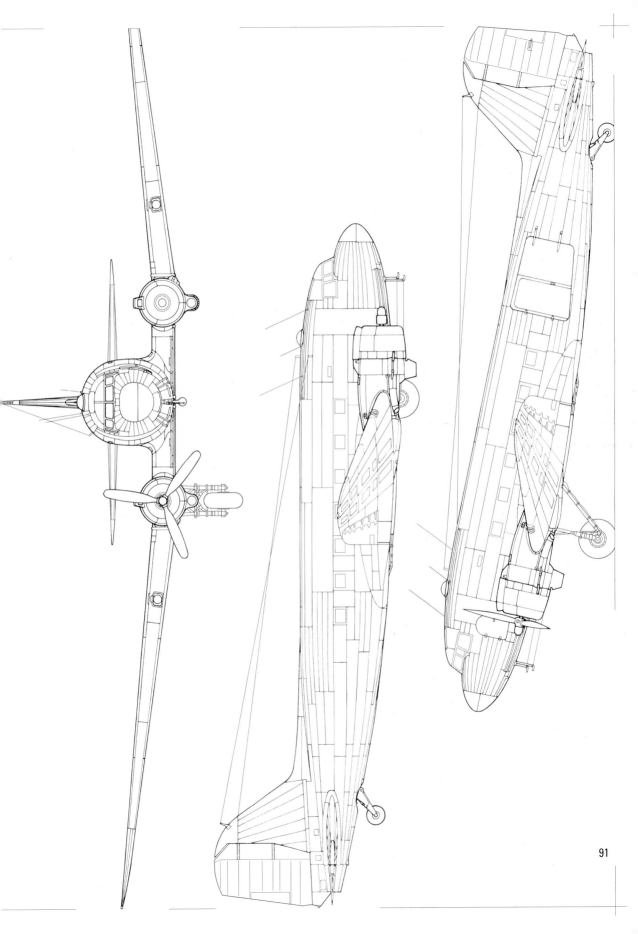

91

COLOUR PLATES

Notes

Most ETO C-47s had a factory-applied forest green over olive drab (OD) pattern. Earlier aircraft (most coming over in 1942 and some in early 1943) had overall OD and neutral gray undersurfaces. Some C-47s received forest green overspray on the undersurfaces as well, but few if any of these seem to have operated in the ETO/MTO. A few transport aircraft in North Africa had 'sand and spinach' uppersurfaces, with neutral gray or light blue undersurfaces.

OD wore differently on different parts of a C-47. The paint on the control surfaces always looked different, even when the aeroplane was brand new. This was due to the different surface reflectivity, but also because the control surfaces were supplied, doped and painted, by a subcontractor. The control surfaces, the fin and the outer wing panels were where the most variation was evident. Some faded OD almost went a light 'milk chocolate' colour. There was often heavy wear near door hinges, showing many different shades of OD and repainting, or reinforcing with tape or sheet metal.

Painted-over invasion stripes were often visible through OD. On a few occasions, C-47s were lost when caught by the Luftwaffe on the ground. It was thought that the invasion stripes on the upper fuselage and wing surfaces were too much of an invitation to such threats, and they were ordered painted out on all C-47s and gliders, leaving only those on the undersurfaces. The removal of these stripes had been carried out on many C-47s before it was officially mandated for *Market-Garden*.

Aircraft in *Anvil-Dragoon* had red spinners and, in some cases, red cowling leading edges as a recognition marking. Other C-47s in the MTO had a variety of unit markings in lieu of the ETO codes, including fuselage and rudder stripes.

After *Market-Garden*, underwing stripes were ordered painted out, leaving only those under the fuselage. All stripes were ordered painted out for Operation *Varsity*. Some units, however, did not get the word, and retained the under-fuselage stripes until VE-Day.

Most, but by no means all, nose art was painted under the cockpit on the pilot's side – he sat on the left. Most often, the inside of the cargo doors was painted zinc chromate green. When scheduled to drop paratroops or supplies, the C-47's jump door was often removed and a number chalked on the fuselage side to direct loading. The 316th TCG and other USAAF units in the MTO whose aircraft bore RAF fin flashes had these painted on with bright US insignia red, white and blue paint.

Natural metal C-47s were largely limited to ATC and NATS, and were usually aircraft that had been through a major overhaul in-theatre. Some of these were re-camouflaged by their units with OD or forest green. Natural metal C-47s were thought to be too conspicuous when operating from forward airstrips.

1
C-49B 41-7693, USAAC, 1941

Used for priority flights pre-war, this aircraft was one of the first pre-war DC-3s to join the USAAC in February 1941. Note its seven airline-style windows and door, plus baggage compartment. The aircraft was sent to Australia to serve with the Fifth Air Force in September 1942, and was handed over to the Royal Australian Air Force in February of the following year. Post-war, it remained in Australia, operating as an airliner until scrapped at Essendon airport, Victoria, on 6 November 1969.

2
C-53 41-20062, 10th TG, Fresno Air Depot, California, 1941

This aircraft features a standard 1941 USAAF transport scheme – overall dark olive drab uppersurfaces and neutral gray undersides, with no green overspray. It also wore pre-war insignia in four positions. The C-53's detail markings consist of aircraft number 62 over 10T on the fin, plus an orange arrow containing the letters *F.A.D* (Fresno Air Depot) on the fuselage. The 10T62 codes were repeated both above and below the wing.

3
R4D-1 BuNo 3131, NAS Patuxtent River, Maryland, early 1942

This early production aircraft was amongst the first C-47s transferred to the Navy as an R4D-1. Marked up in standard USAAF camouflage, the transport has Navy-style rudder stripes (red and white only, with no blue vertical bar). Delivered to NAS Anacostia in February 1942, it spent much of the war serving with the Marine Corps prior to being struck off charge in April 1946.

4
C-53-DO 41-20090, ATC, 1942

Operated on the northern route by Northeast Airlines in 1942, this aircraft was regularly flown by Capt Alva Marsh.

5
C-47-DL 41-38576, Accra, Gold Coast, 1942

One of the first C-47s to see action against Germany, this aircraft flew priority spare parts and other cargo that had been brought by fast ship (or aircraft) from West Africa to Egypt, saving the long voyage around the Cape of Good Hope.
Delivered to the USAAF in June 1942, it eventually wound up in India with the Tenth Air Force and was sold to the Indian government in April 1946.

6
C-47-DL 41-18608, 60th TCG, Huntingdon, Cambridgeshire, October 1942

Delivered to the Eighth Air Force in late October 1942, this aircraft remained with the 60th TCG until it was withdrawn from use on 31 October 1944.

7
C-47-DL 41-18376 *MISS CARRIAGE*, 64th TCG, Ramsbury, Wiltshire, November 1942
MISS CARRIAGE had the distinction of dropping the same British paratroopers from 3 Para twice – once in *Torch* and in *Fustian*. The yellow roundel ring appeared on the fuselage insignia only, and the aircraft's antennas were limited to stub VHF receivers on the port side aft of the astrodome. Serving with both the Eighth and Twelfth Air Forces, 41-18376 was sold into civilian hands in 1946 and migrated to Colombia, where it still remains airworthy.

8
R4D-3 '7-R-51' (BuNo unknown), VR-7, Naval Air Transport Service, Rio de Janeiro, Brazil, April 1943
Flown by Lt(jg) Carl Vietor, this aircraft is typical of the many R4D-3s used in the ETO/MTO in 1943-44.

9
C-47-DL 41-18527 *JIMINY CRICKET*, 36th TCS/316th TCG, Enfidaville, Tunisia, 11 July 1943
Flown by 2Lt G B Quisenberry, this aircraft is depicted as it appeared for the Sicily operation in improvised night camouflage. It was one of the original 52 C-47s that deployed to Egypt with the 316th TCG in December 1942. Transferred to Ninth Air Force control in the Netherlands in late October 1944, 41-18527 was scrapped in January 1947

10
C-47-DL 41-38592, 316th TCG, Enfidaville, Tunisia, 1943
The 316th TCG retained the RAF fin flash on its C-47s until 1944. It also had national insignia in six positions, RAF style, rather than the usual five as per USAAF regulations. Serving with the Twelfth Air Force through to VE-Day, this C-47 appeared on the US civil register until sold to the French Air Force in April 1957. It was scrapped in 1971.

11
R4D-5 '1-R-152' (BuNo unknown), VR-1, NATS, Rio de Janeiro, Brazil, August 1943
This Navy R4D-5 was used on the southern route to Africa in 1943. Unlike most R4Ds, it has been repainted in Navy colours. Its ADF antenna takes the form of a loop under the fuselage. The R4Ds serving with FAW-7/15 were painted either in standard OD/gray or in this Navy scheme. The Navy HQ detachment at Hendon used ex-TCC C-47s with their code numbers and personal markings obscured with fresh OD or green paint.

12
C-49K (ex-DC-3-G202A NC30038 c/n 6340), North Atlantic Wing, ATC, Presque Island, Maine, October 1943
This is a standard DC-3 in military markings, hence its lack of a C-47-style cargo door. It features the pre-war underwing *U.S. ARMY* titling long after it should have been painted out. Its yellow rudder, fuselage band, cowling and sideways diamond insignia on the nose were markings frequently seen on ATC aircraft. Note the previous yellow fuselage band covered over in medium green (including under belly, painted over in medium green not in neutral gray). The aircraft also features the ATC insignia on the yellow fuselage band.

13
C-53D-DO 42-68850, General Officer Commanding British Eighth Army, Cairo, 4 March 1944
The highest-ranking British commanders often acquired USAAF transports and crews, and as such, this was the personal aircraft of Gen Oliver Leese, GOC Eighth Army. Christened *Lilli Marlene*, it was later taken to the CBI, where the aircraft sprouted an external name (which it lacked in Cairo).

14
C-47A 42-24046, 320th TS/27th TG, Warton, Lancashire, May 1944
This aircraft was the favourite of the author's father during his time at Warton, 'Old 46' having joined the 27th TG from North Africa in early 1944. It was highly reliable, which accounts for its longevity – the aircraft is still flying on the British civil register.

15
C-47A-80-DL 43-15159 *The Argonia*, 94th TCS/439th TCG, Upottery, Devon, 5-6 June 1944
The Argonia (named after its pilot's Kansas home town) was the 439th's lead aeroplane for Operation *Overlord*, being flown by group CO, Col Charles H Young. The C-47's individual aircraft number, in black on a light grey disc, also appeared on the aircraft's starboard upper wing – this was only done by the 439th TCG for D-Day. *The Argonia* had an SCR-717C antenna under the belly. As with most IX TCC C-47s, after D-Day 43-15159 acquired a scoreboard and gradually shed its invasion stripes.

16
C-47A-65-DL 42-100521 *KILROY IS HERE*, 92nd TCS/439th TCG, Upottery, Devon, 6 June 1944
Seen in typical D-Day finish, this aircraft has OD uppersurfaces (with medium green overspray), full invasion stripes, light grey (lighter than neutral gray) squadron codes and aircraft letter and a yellow serial. This machine survived the war and appeared on the US civil register in the late 1940s.

17
C-47A-30-DK 43-47981, 492nd BG, Harrington, Northamptonshire, 7 June 1944
This aircraft was flown by Col Cliff Heflin to Ain, in France, on 7 June 1944. A 'Carpetbaggers' machine (hence no D-Day stripes), it would land in France to pick up evaders and French resistance personnel.

18
C-47A-50-DL 42-24190 *Sugar Puss*, 90th TCS/438th TCG, Greenham Common, Berkshire, 7 June 1944
Depicted as it appeared for Mission 'Elmira', this aircraft was crewed that day by Lt Gib Estelle (pilot), Lt Marcus Portzline (co-pilot), Sgt Gordon Jacobs (radio) and Sgt Porto (crew chief). Damaged by flak,

Sugar Puss made it to RAF Warmwell after Sgt Porto spliced leaking fuel lines in flight. He was awarded the DFC for his efforts. Note the name *"Emily"* in script (and quotation marks) on the port engine cowling. Used throughout the 1944-45 campaign, *Sugar Puss* acquired a scoreboard and incrementally lost its invasion stripes. Sold into civilian hands post-war, the aircraft spent time on the US, Canadian and Peruvian registers.

19
C-47A-75-DL 42-100847, 91st TCS/439th TCG, Upottery, Devon, 17 September 1944
Flown by 1Lt Don LePard during the airborne drop at Groesbeek, this aircraft, in standard markings for the period, had the number 2 chalked on its side under the aft window. This was used as an identifying mark by paratroops loading on the ground, and written in chalk, it usually blew away in flight. Note the hasty painting out of the invasion stripes.

20
R4D-5 BuNo 17101, VR-1, NATS, NAS Argentia, Newfoundland, October 1944
Flown by Lt Morris and Lt(jg) B J Rokkan, this all-metal R4D was used in 1944-45 by NATS on the North Atlantic route, supporting US Navy ships in Newfoundland, Iceland and the UK. It features the colourful NATS nose insignia, and also has airline-style fuselage titling. The R4D's 1944 fit included an under-fuselage ADF 'football' (in place of the loop as seen on most R4Ds) and a stub upper fuselage VHF antenna on the port side, aft of the astrodome.

21
C-47A-20-DK 42-93255, 10th TCS/60th TCG, 51st TCW, Megara, Greece, 12 October 1944
This newly-delivered C-47A, equipped with SCR-717C radar, flew as a lead ship in Operation *Manna* – it carried troops from 11 Para. The aircraft was later used in the Balkans and northern Italy.

22
C-47-DL 41-38607 *JACKPOT,* Headquarters Flight, Base Air Depot (BAD) 2, Warton, Lancashire, November 1944
Flown by base commander Col Paul Jackson as a his personal transport, this natural metal early production C-47 had been rebuilt by BAD 2 from a 'war weary' aircraft for use by its own headquarters flight. Such rebuilt aircraft were used by many depots and service groups. 41-38607 had initially served in East and North Africa, before transferring to Eighth Air Force control in February 1944. Ending the war with the Ninth Air Force, the C-47 served as and airliner in France until scrapped in the 1970s.

23
C-47A-65-DL 42-100533 *Honeybun III*, 80th TCS/436th TCG, Membury, Berkshire, early 1945
42-100533 was a re-camouflaged natural metal aeroplane that was likely used for second-line duties by its French-based unit. It went on to serve in the Berlin Airlift, before being scrapped in 1950.

24
C-47A-25-DK 42-93607, 79th TCS/436th TCG, Melun, France, March 1945
Wearing partially stripped invasion stripes, this SCR-717C radar-equipped machine has sheet metal reinforcing around its main cargo door hinges. Flown in Operation *Varsity*, 42-93607 later served its country in a more clandestine way when it was transferred from the USAF to Air America in July 1966. On 22 March 1968, the aircraft was written off when it veered off the runway at Gia Nghia, in South Vietnam, and rolled down an embankment.

25
C-47B-1-DL 43-16389 *Stuka* CHASER, 75th TCS/435th TCG, Bretigny, France, April 1945
Flown by Maj Edgar A Smith, this C-47 captured a formation of Stukas, and their crews, hence the kill markings. It is believed to have been the only USAAF C-47 in the ETO to boast kill markings.

26
C-47A-10-DK 42-92728 *"EIGHTBALL CHARLIE"*, 440th TCG/96th TCS, Orleans-Bricy, France, April 1945
Flown by 1Lt Ray Ottomann, who described it as 'a valiant bird', this C-47 took part in most major operations flown by Troop Carrier units from D-Day to VE-Day. Perhaps its most significant mission was the towing of a glider that contained a volunteer surgical team to Bastogne on 25 December 1944.

27
C-47B-10-DK 43-49258 *"LADY HELEN"*, ATC/MATS, Poltava, Ukraine, April 1945
This newly-built aircraft was damaged in a fuelling accident at Poltava on 30 April 1945.

28
C-47A-90-DL 43-15992 ATC, Orly, Paris, spring 1945
The white diamond and 5992 stencilling on the nose of this machine was typical of ATC C-47s – such nose numbers had spread to troop carrier and transport groups by 1945. Note also the small ATC insignia. This aircraft later became a VC-47A.

29
C-47B-1-DK 43-48474, 312th FS/27th TG, Villacoublay, France, spring 1945
The yellow and black stripes on this machine served as the 27th TG's unit markings. The late build C-47 also boasted elaborate nose art.

30
C-47B-1-DK 43-48247 *VANDRA* MIN VÄG, 86th TS/27th TG, Kierkenes, Norway, January-August 1945
Flown by Col Bernt Balchen, this C-47 was one of ten based at Kallax, in Sweden, ferrying Norwegian troops to Kierkenes and other bases in northern Norway, as well as providing logistics support and casualty evacuation. Its Swedish name translates as 'Going My Way' (from the Bing Crosby film). The squadron insignia is of George Baker's classic cartoon character 'The Sad Sack', heavily laden.

BIBLIOGRAPHY

Archival Material
US National Archives, RG 18, Entry 7, TCW/TCG/TCS files
US National Archives, RG 342.2, Unit history files
US National Archives, RG 331, FAAA files
US Army Military History Institute document collection
US Air Force Historical Research Agency files

Operations
Roger E Bilstein, *Airlift and Airborne Operations in World War II*, Washington, 1998, Government Printing Office
Ronald G Boston, 'Doctrine By Default: The Historical Origins of Tactical Airlift', *Air University Review*, May-June 1983
Wesley Craven & James Cate, *The Army Air Forces in World War II*, Washington, 1983, Air Force Historical Agency reprint, vols 1-3, 7
Philip Esvelin, *D-Day Gliders,* Bayeux, 2001, Heimdal
Lewis E Johnson, *The Troop Carrier D-Day Flights,* San Francisco, 2002, self-published
HQ IX TCC, *Supply By Air*, 20 November 1944. USNARA, RG 18, Entry 7, Box 120, Operational Reports File
Robert F Futrell, *Development of Aeromedical Evacuation in the USAF, vol. I,* USAF Historical Study No 23, Maxwell AFB, 1961, USAF Historical Research Agency
Marten, Lawrence M, *Fighters or Freighters?,* thesis, University of Nebraska, 1993
Rex Shama, *Pulse and Repulse*, Austin, 1995, Eakin
Harris G Warren*, Special Operations: AAF Aid to European Resistance Movements,* USAF Historical Study No 121, Maxwell AFB, 1947, USAF Historical Research Agency
John C Warren, Airborne *Missions in the European Theater 1942-45*, USAF Historical Study No 97, Maxwell AFB, 1956, USAF Historical Research Agency
John C Warren, *Airborne Missions in the Mediterranean Theater 1942-45,* USAF Historical Study No 74, Maxwell AFB, September 1955, USAF Historical Research Agency
Bo Widfeldt, 'Operation Ball', *Air Enthusiast* 12, April-July 1980
Williams, Brig Gen Paul, Memoranda on Sicily operations in USAFHRA files 532.452A, 611.719, and 613.01

Reference
Kit C Carter & Robert Mueller, *Combat Chronology* 1941-45, Washington, 1991, Center for Air Force History
J M G Gadidge, *The Douglas DC-3 and its Predecessors*, Tonbridge, Kent, 1984, Air Britain
Vic Flintham and Andrew Thomas, *Combat Codes*, Shrewsbury, 2003, Airlife
Rene Francillon, *McDonnell Douglas Aircraft Since 1920*, V I, London, 1988, Putnam
HQ, Army Air Forces, *Army Air Forces Statistical Digest*, December 1945
Maurer M, *Air Force Combat Units of World War II*, Washington, 1961, US Government Printing Office
Maurer M, *Air Force Combat Squadrons of World War II*, Washington, 1969, US Government Printing Office

Histories
Roger A Freeman, *The Ninth Air Force in Colour*, London, 1995, Arms & Armour
John F Hamlin, *Support & Strike*, Peterborough, 1991, GMS
David Polk, *World War II Army Airborne Troop Carriers*, Paducah, 1992, Turner Publishing
Kenn Rust, *The Ninth Air Force in World War II,* Fallbrook CA, 1970, Aero

Units
W L Brinson & George Cholewczynski, *Three One Five Group*, New Orleans, Walka, 2003
Austin J Buchanan, *The 438th Troop Carrier Group in World War II*, Baldwin MI, 1990, self-published
Robert E Callahan, *On Wings of Troop Carriers in World War II*, San Antonio, 1997, Burke (50th TCS/314thTCG)
Frank Guild Jr, *Action of the Tiger*, Nashville, Battery Press, 1978 (437th TCG)
Joseph Harkiewicz, *We Are the 29th[th]*, 1990 [29 TCS], 1990, Orlando, self-published.
Don Haffeman, ed. *313th Troop Carrier Group - 47th Troop Carrier Squadron Historical Diary*, Skokie IL, 1978, Intercollegiate Press
Michael Ingrisano Jr, *Valor Without Arms, A History of the 316th TCG, 1942-45*, 2001, Bennington VT, Merriam Press
F X Krebs, *DZ Europe, The Story of the 440th TCG*, 2nd ed., Tallahassee, 2003, 440th TCG Memorial Project
Jon A Maguire, *Gooney Birds and Ferry Tales. The 27th Air Transport Group in World War II*, 1998, Atglen PA, Schiffer
Donald L Van Reken, *The 32nd Troop Carrier Squadron*, 1989, Holland MI, self-published
Martin Wolfe, *Green Light* (81st TCS), Washington, 1993, Center for Air Force History
Charles H Young, *Into the Valley*, 1995 (439th TCG), Dallas, 1995, PrintComm
Yuhasz, Joseph & Rosemary, *History of the Fifteenth Troop Carrier Squadron*, Midvale UT, 1994, self-published
Invaders, Paris, 1945, Defosses-Novogravure (50th TCW)

INDEX

References to illustrations are shown in **bold**. Plates are shown with page and caption locators in brackets, with 'insignia' plates having an 'I' prefix.